STRANGERS

STRANGERS

A MEMOIR OF

MARRIAGE

Belle Burden

THE DIAL PRESS

New York

Hardcover ISBN 978-0-593-73331-8
Ebook ISBN 978-0-593-73332-5

Printed in the United States of America on acid-free paper

1st Printing

FIRST EDITION

BOOK TEAM: PRODUCTION EDITOR: *Andy Lefkowitz* •
MANAGING EDITOR: *Rebecca Berlant* • PRODUCTION MANAGER: *Sandra Sjursen* •
COPY EDITOR: *Mark McCauslin* • PROOFREADERS: *Kimberly Broderick,
Brandon Hopkins, Megha Jain, and Brianna Lopez*

Book design by Barbara M. Bachman

The authorized representative in the EU for product safety and compliance
is Penguin Random House Ireland, Morrison Chambers, 32 Nassau Street,
Dublin D02 YH68, Ireland. https://eu-contact.penguin.ie

FOR MY CHILDREN

This book is the story of my marriage, its ending, and what happened afterward. It recounts events as accurately as I can remember them. I have used my own name and the real names of my grandparents, parents, stepmother, brother, and sister-in-law. I have changed all other names. In some cases, I have also changed identifying details.

Part I

Each spring, an osprey couple returns to the same nest on our property on Martha's Vineyard. The nest is on the edge of a lake that leads into the Vineyard Sound, facing west. In lucky years, eggs appear in the nest in May, chicks in June. In July, the juvenile ospreys learn to fly. By September, the family is gone, headed to the Caribbean or South America for the winter.

When we bought our house in 2005, my husband, James, became obsessed with the osprey couple, with the magic of their annual return to the same location. He was always anxious, waiting to see if they would appear, if they would produce eggs, if the eggs would survive raccoons and crows, our local predators. Every year, he celebrated when the juveniles flew for the first time.

He drew me and our three young children into the drama of the ospreys, pointing them out as they soared above us, leading us in yelling "Hi, Ossey!" and waving at the sky. He took us into the woods to see their nest wedged high in a tree. He befriended two local osprey experts, older men who invited us to watch them tag an osprey at dawn.

They attached a device that would track the bird's movements during the winter. The kids, still in their pajamas, were awestruck by the creature that looked so much larger on the ground than it did in the sky. The experts named the tagged osprey after me and sent us updates on Belle's progress throughout the winter. We worried for her and toasted her return.

After raccoons ravaged the ospreys' eggs two years in a row, the experts installed a pole in the same area as the original nest, designed to deter climbing animals. The tree stayed empty for a few years and then, to our astonishment, a small nest appeared. The nest grew steadily, becoming more majestic every summer, a landmark visible to swimmers and boaters across the lake. After a decade, it measured more than four feet wide and three feet tall, one of the biggest nests on the island.

When we arrived on the Vineyard in March of 2020, the nest was empty. The birds were still warming themselves in the southern hemisphere, perhaps beginning their pilgrimage back to the island, making their way over the Caribbean Sea and Florida, continuing north, hugging the coastline, as a virus, first found in China, made its own explosive journey through the United States. My husband and I walked around the pole in our wool hats and parkas, our boots sinking in the marsh. The nest was intact, unchanged from the previous fall. Even in the bitter air, even with sharp sticks poking out of every side, it looked strong and stable. Welcoming. We smiled at each other and talked about the couple's return. *Would we be here to see it?*

———

After the COVID-19 pandemic shuttered New York City, where we lived most of the year, we decided to quarantine on Martha's Vineyard with our two youngest children, then fifteen and twelve. It made sense to move to the Vineyard; our house there was isolated and it was our favorite place in the world. The hedge fund where James worked had gone remote, and my legal work could be done from anywhere.

We arrived on March 15. The island was still firmly in winter, with temperatures in the thirties, the trees barren, and the light flat. An icy wind whipped around us as we unloaded the car, unpacking sweaters and boots, the girls' textbooks and cellos, one larger than the other. James set up his home office on a card table in the living room, rising at 4 a.m. to worry over the markets. He cut three different kinds of wood and built gorgeous fires in the late afternoon. He made me whiskey sours as the sun set (we believed reports that whiskey would kill the virus) and locked every door of the house at night, even though the island's population was sparse and, like New York, in lockdown. He seemed proud of his role as father and husband, nurturing us, protecting us.

I went for walks, tried to keep up with house cleaning and laundry, and watched the news throughout the day. There were images of overflowing emergency rooms, hospital tents in Central Park, refrigerated trucks filled with corpses. More than 20,000 people had died in New York City. There was no vaccine, and no timeline for one. Even in our isolation, even with our privilege, I was afraid.

I often sought out James in the woods. Out of our daughters' earshot, we would talk about the latest pandemic news, whether we should wear masks or gloves to the grocery store, if we needed to isolate grocery bags and packages before we unpacked them. James would kiss the top of my head as I hugged him, gripping the back of his sweater.

Our younger daughter, Carrie, discovered Fortnite and played remote games with her friends in our guest bedroom, her small body dwarfed by a giant armchair. Our older daughter, Evie, wanted to learn to make fresh pasta. She started with gnocchi and served it for dinner on March 21, the first night of spring. James made a roast chicken to accompany Evie's dish, using our outdoor grill as an oven, standing on our deck in the dark, adjusting the knobs, making sure the temperature stayed at four hundred degrees. It came out perfectly: moist and golden brown.

We ate at our rectangular wooden table in the kitchen. I wore pajamas with a thick wool sweater and socks, my hair still wet from the shower, piled into a bun on the top of my head. The wind howled as we ate. James seemed distracted and kept eating the gnocchi directly from the bowl rather than serving himself, a pet peeve of mine. He removed the oyster from the chicken, the piece he'd taught the kids to covet, and gave it to Carrie.

I FaceTimed our son, Finn, who was staying with his friend's family on Long Island, joining a group of teenagers. At seventeen, we knew he would be happier with his friends, and we thought his time away from us would be limited, a couple of weeks at most. I held up my phone so we could all see his face. We told him we missed him.

After we finished eating, James left the kitchen to make a work call. The girls went to the living room to watch television. Alone, I soaked the pans, loaded the dishwasher, wiped down the table. As I was filling a bucket with water and white vinegar to mop the floor, my cell phone rang, glowing and vibrating on the kitchen island. I didn't recognize the number, so I let it go to voicemail. When my phone pinged to register the message, I put down the bucket and pressed play. It was a man's voice. He sounded young and nervous.

He said, "I'm trying to reach Belle." He paused. "I'm sorry to tell you this, but your husband is having an affair with my wife." He gave his name and number.

I froze, feeling dizzy. The words didn't make sense. I gripped my phone and pressed the play arrow again, listening to the man's soft voice for the second time. I thought, *This can't be true. This must be a mistake. James will explain this.*

I leaned the mop against the island and went to find him, descending our stairs just as he ascended them. He was coming to find me. He looked anxious, worried.

He put his hand on the small of my back and guided me into the guest bedroom, the room set up with Fortnite, with empty packets of Cheddar Bunnies on the rug. He sat down on the couch. I sat in a chair to his right. There was a long pause, as if he was collecting his thoughts, searching for the right words to make this go away. I thought he would do that—he would make it go away. I waited.

He took both my hands, leaned forward, and looked me straight in the eye. He said, "I promise you, this meant nothing. It's over. I love you and only you. I'm so sorry. I'm so embarrassed."

I asked, "How long has it been going on?"

He answered, "Only a few weeks."

I looked down at his hands, at my body, and felt ashamed of my matronly pajamas and my socks, an oil stain from dinner on the thin cotton of my pajama pants.

His platinum wedding band, on his ring finger, looked scuffed from years of wear. My fingers, underneath his, were bare. I had taken off my rings, including my diamond wedding band, the day before. A friend had told me that the virus could hide under rings, evading Purell and soap, so I had pulled them off, dropping them in a jar of jewelry cleaner. For a split second I thought, *Did taking off my wedding ring cause this? Did I shake something loose in the universe?*

"What is her name?" I asked.

"It doesn't matter," he said.

"I'm going to call her husband back, so you might as well tell me."

He said the name. It was generic and, like my maiden name, alliterative; it sounded sweet.

"Where did you meet her?" I asked.

He said she was a banker. They'd met through work. He said, "We had this attraction."

He pulled his hands from mine and held them up to demonstrate the force pulling them together, his hands cupped, fingers spread, like he was holding a basketball. "But, I swear, it didn't mean anything."

"Does she have children?" I asked.

He nodded and said, "She has two kids."

"How old are they?"

He paused and said, "They are little. How old are kids when they go to nursery school?"

"Two or three."

He nodded again. "That's how old they are."

I thought, *How does a woman with a big job and two toddlers have the time, the energy, for an affair?*

Carrie called for me, "Mommy? Can you make us turnovers?"

I jumped, hearing her high, sweet voice reorienting me. *The girls.* We would need to pretend everything was fine, that a bomb had not just exploded.

I called back, "Okay."

I left James in the guest room and returned to the kitchen. I turned on the oven and set two frozen Pepperidge Farm raspberry turnovers on a baking sheet. My kids had loved them since they were little. I had too, as a child. I put the sheet in the oven.

No longer able to contain what felt like a rising explosion, I walked to our bathroom, stepped into our shower, and closed the glass door to muffle my gasps, my wails. I sat down on the shower bench, between the shampoos and soaps, and texted the man who had called me, "Can you tell me how long this has been going on?"

It felt like the most important thing in that moment—to know when the affair started, to know if James had told me the truth.

He responded, "I think a month. But I can't text because my wife has tried to kill herself. She's in an ambulance."

I felt panic then. James's betrayal was going to cause waves of damage beyond me, beyond our family. This was a crisis we would need to manage together. I began to worry too, for the young woman in the ambulance, speeding through the empty streets of New York, undone by what had transpired that night, in her house and mine, as if she were my daughter and not my husband's mistress.

I left the bathroom and went to find James again, moving through the living room and down the stairs, wanting to relay the news quickly, as if my speed might save her. I found him standing outside the guest room. He was on his cell phone.

I knew, somehow, that he was talking to her. I asked, "Do you know?"

He put his hand over his phone and said, "Yes. I'm trying to hear what she is saying."

I waited as he walked away from me, into the guest room, to finish the call. His posture—the hunch of his back, his free hand cupped over his mouth—looked intimate, caretaking.

When he came back, putting the phone into his pocket, he said, "She took a few sleeping pills. She's fine." He looked relieved.

My sympathy, my worry, shifted to astonishment. *She had taken the pills the moment I—James's wife of two decades—had learned about her? Wasn't I the one who was supposed to fall apart? Wasn't he supposed to be worried about me?* She had captured my husband's attention, his care, when I needed it most.

I don't remember exactly how I spent the next hours.

I know I took the turnovers out of the oven. They had cooked too long, becoming too crisp, too brown.

I know I returned to the bathroom.

I know I called my stepmother, Susan, and told her what had happened. She yelped in shock. While I was on the phone with her, Evie knocked softly on the door. The doorknob turned slowly, cautiously, and then stopped. I had locked it.

"Are you okay, Mom?" she called through the door.

I steadied my voice, raising it an octave. "Yes, sweetheart, I'm fine. A friend is going through something." She told me later that James had sent her to the bathroom. He had said, "Go check on Mommy."

I texted two close friends, Maria and Anna, "James is having an affair."

They both answered immediately, confused, writing "What??" They called me in succession. I didn't answer.

I curled into a ball on the cold tile and stayed there for a long time. I imagined the weeks ahead in lockdown, keeping things stable for the girls, doing therapy with James on Zoom. We were stuck together, in the same house, on an island. I thought, *This is going to be a nightmare.* I could not imagine forgiving him, but I also could not imagine a life without him; I loved him so completely.

At 3 a.m., I walked through the quiet house and found James sleeping in Finn's bed. He looked peaceful, breathing steadily, like nothing was wrong. The girls were asleep in their room next door, both turned to the wall in their twin beds, under their matching yellow-and-white-flowered duvets. I hadn't put Carrie to bed, something I still did every night. I thought, *She must have been happy, staying up past her bedtime, assuming I had forgotten.*

I went back to our room and got in our bed, James's side undisturbed. I tried to sleep but couldn't. I felt leaden with dread. The scenes of the night kept replaying in my mind—the voicemail, James's admission and apology, the suicide attempt—and I could not make sense of it. I could not place what had happened with what I knew of my husband, a kind and mild man, a devoted husband and father. I hadn't drawn the curtains, so I saw the sun rise over the lake. I could tell it would be a beautiful day, crisp and sunny.

At 6 a.m., James walked into our bedroom fully dressed, in heavy boots and a black parka, the same clothes he'd worn the night before. He was holding a large canvas tote bag. His green eyes were narrowed and icy, an expression I had never seen before, entirely different from how he had looked at me the previous night. Before he said a word, I knew that something, everything, had changed.

He said, "I've decided I want a divorce. I'm leaving."

As he spoke, I could not absorb what was happening, what he was saying. I thought the end (or the survival) of our marriage would be my choice.

He said, "You'll be fine. You're still young." I was fifty.

I asked, "Are you going to see her?"

He said, "Yes, I would like to make sure she is okay."

I told him that her name did not appear on her firm's website. I had done a google search and thought, maybe illogically, the whole thing could be a scam. He scrolled through his phone and showed me an announcement of her recent promotion. She had an impressive résumé, including a degree from an Ivy League business school. He looked proud, impressed. And then he walked out the door.

———

The girls were still asleep when he left. When I heard their movements, their steps on the stairs, my door opening, I pulled back James's side of the duvet to make it look like he had slept there. They got in bed with me, warm in their matching monkey-print pajamas, their hair tousled with sleep. I tried to smile as they curled against me, hoping I could hide the red blotches on my face.

I said, "Daddy had to go back to New York for work."

Carrie asked, "Why didn't he say goodbye?"

I paused, trying to find an answer. "He was in a rush to make the first ferry."

I called James repeatedly over the next five hours, while he was on the road, but he didn't answer. He called back when he reached New York. I could hear him park the car in the garage, hand the keys to the attendant, walk down the street.

He said, "I thought I was happy but I'm not. I thought I wanted our life, but I don't."

He said, "I feel like a switch has flipped. I'm done."

He said, "You can have the house and the apartment. You can have custody of the kids. I don't want it. I don't want any of it."

Of all the words he said, it was *custody* and *house* that took my breath away. *He was giving up our kids? And the Vineyard?* This was not just an affair. This was not just a rejection of me. He was abandoning all of it, and all of us.

———

In the days that followed, I continued to try to hide the truth from the girls. A therapist I spoke with said I should wait to tell them until the pandemic was less scary. It was still March, the second week of lockdown. We thought it would be over soon. Or at least that the worst of it—the deaths, the shutdown, the unknowns—would end.

But instead of easing, the pandemic had become more frightening. And so had I, appearing at dinner with swollen eyes and unwashed hair. I cried quietly as I did laundry and scrubbed our toilets. I spent hours behind the closed door of my bedroom. I decided not to drink, knowing it would make me sadder, but I also found it hard to eat, my appetite disappearing, my throat thick.

I called James every few hours, in closets, bathrooms, the garage, the woods, anywhere the girls couldn't hear me, crying in heavy jags, begging for some explanation. He was always nearly silent. He wouldn't tell me what was lacking in our marriage or in me, or how long he had felt this way. He denied that it was because he was in love, a reason that would have hurt but at least made some sense. When he spoke, he was completely calm, his voice low. His composure made me feel like I was wrong to be upset, to be so messy and confused, like what was happening was something I should absorb quickly and easily.

I never asked him to change his mind. I knew that this was not possible; he was too certain. But I wanted him to at least try to walk me through his decision, for him to show some concern for me and the kids, even if he was leaving. He gave me nothing. It was like a wall had been erected between us, me on one side flailing in my despair; him on the other, cold as ice.

His only answers were "I don't know." And once, "You didn't do anything wrong." I begged him to do therapy with me on Zoom. He refused. And then he stopped answering my phone calls.

He texted, "I'll answer what I want, when I want. I'll speak when I want. I'll decide when I want."

Had life been normal, had we been in New York, had I been able to find him on the street and make him look me in the eye, maybe I would have some understanding of what was happening. But I was on one island, and he was on another, and I knew nothing, only the shock of his disappearance.

I texted him, "I think I'm going to die."

He didn't answer.

In the middle of one night, I became convinced that he had fathered the toddlers, the children of the woman with the alliterative name. In my shock and disorientation, even this seemed possible. When I called him at 1 a.m., he answered, the late hour taking him off guard. I said, "Are they yours?"

He answered, "Stop. You have lost your mind." And then he hung up the phone.

I felt like I *had* lost my mind, like his exit had transformed me, suddenly, from an intelligent, stable wife and mother to an unhinged lunatic. A madwoman. Somehow, I had become the dangerous person in the story, the volatile character, rather than he, the man who had left his family.

While he refused to talk to me on the phone, he sent one clear message by text: he planned to tell people that our separation was amicable, a joint decision. He said it would be better, for my own well-being, to say that I had wanted it too.

He assumed I would agree to this false narrative. His expectation made sense. In most things, for twenty years, I had deferred to him. I believed in his wisdom, that he knew the right answer. I tend to be a compliant person generally. I didn't break a single rule in school. I was an obedient daughter, a diligent lawyer. My older brother loved to call me "Belle the Good." I am also shy, private, and avoidant of confrontation. I didn't talk at all until I was three years old, and I rarely spoke as a child after that. Every teacher comment on every report card, from kindergarten through college, noted that while bright and performing well, I needed to say more in class. Whenever I did speak, my face would turn bright red. As an adult, I learned how to make small talk but stayed quiet, remote, sharing my intimate thoughts and problems with only a few close friends.

For what felt like the first time, I refused James's advice. I replied, "No. I won't say that."

I would not lie about this, about what was happening to me. This boundary felt clear to me, even in my confusion, even in my despair.

James refused to tell his own family—his mother, brother, and sister—that he had left us, so I told them, sending an email two days after his departure. They were upset and worried. His brother, sister, and I texted back and forth throughout the first bleak days, trying to figure out what

had happened, as if this were a puzzle we could solve together. James's sister was outraged by the LinkedIn photo of
the woman James was seeing; she was thirty-five but looked
twenty. She tracked down the woman's parents, trying, un-
successfully, to stop the affair.

And then, suddenly, on April 1, eight days after James
walked out, his family cut me off. In a joint text, his siblings
said that in order to support James, they could no longer
be in contact with me. The bluntness of the message, their
coldness matching James's, stunned me. I'd been a part of
their family for twenty years.

———

Carrie didn't seem to sense anything was wrong. She was a
child who saw only what was in front of her—her classes on
Zoom, a TikTok dance, her Fortnite games. She arrived at
the table ready to eat, not caring what her sister and I gave
her, as long as it was piping hot. She accepted the story that
her father was working, even though all of Manhattan was
shut down.

Evie texted me in the middle of the night, a few days after
James left, saying something cryptic about how she knew
I had a lot on my plate, that I shouldn't worry about her.
When I read the text in the morning, I went to find her, my
heart beating fast. I didn't know what I would say to her. She
was still in bed, alone in the girls' yellow room. I sat down
at her feet.

I said, "Can we talk about your text?"

She answered softly, "No, it's fine."

"What did you mean by it?"

"Mom, please, it's fine, I don't want to talk right now." Her voice was firm now, definitive. She pulled up the duvet and rolled over, turning away from me.

I thought, *Should I press her? Should I insist on an answer? What if she doesn't know?*

I waited a few more minutes, hoping she would give me some kind of signal, some direction, but we both remained silent.

She started cooking for us almost every night. I thought it was a new passion, an expansion of her interest in pasta making. I know now that she was trying to feed me. She made risotto with saffron and used the leftover rice to make arancini the next day. She baked homemade falafel and served it with hummus, warm pita bread, Israeli salad. She perfected a pan-seared steak, learning how to spoon butter and thyme over it as it cooked. She found a Bolognese recipe on Instagram that was much better than mine. She watched me carefully as I ate. I tried to take a few bites of the meals she placed in front of me, even though I felt no hunger.

I called the parents Finn was staying with, people I had never met, and told them what had happened. They were separated, on their way to divorce, but living together during lockdown. They promised to keep my secret until I was ready to tell Finn. By April, they had almost a dozen kids staying with them, a group they called their "quaran-teens." They made sure Finn attended Zoom school, ate well, and got some exercise. The mother taught him to do his laundry. The father worried over his sleep apnea and ordered him a special pillow from Amazon.

When I thought about Finn so far away, I felt a deep ache.

I yearned to have him under my roof, to have my eyes on all three of my children. But I was also relieved that he was not with us, that he wasn't stuck in a house of girls, a house that felt heavy with sadness, without any of his friends. And that he was protected, for a time, from knowing that his father was no longer there.

I tried to get through each hour, each long day. Lockdown meant that no one in my family, none of my close friends, could get to me. No one could pick me up off the bathroom floor. No one could enter the house in a friendly bluster, distracting the girls with games or movies. No one could sit with me on the couch and grip my arm as I recounted what had happened. I do not like the phone; as a shy person, it makes me anxious. But it was my only lifeline.

When I told my mother, calling her from the garage the first morning after James left, she was outraged, and fierce in her defense of me. She had always loved James, but she had experience in the end of relationships, the end of marriages, the disappointment of unfaithful men. To her it was not murky. She said, "You must cut him out of your heart, like a cancer."

My brother, Carter, and his wife, Charmaine, called often, both shocked that James had cheated on me, that he had left us during lockdown. My brother said, "Give him time. I'm sure he will come back."

Two friends called me early every morning. Anna, a friend from boarding school, worried for me as one would a sister. We had known each other for thirty-five years, having met in our small dorm when I was fifteen and she was fourteen. She was compassionate and wise, her personality completely authentic, with no channel for falseness. When I heard her voice asking gently, "How do you feel today?" I knew she really wanted to know, that she would wait and listen. Our conversations often lasted for over an hour, beginning as early as 6 a.m., continuing as the sun rose.

A friend from Brooklyn also called early, never missing a morning. She was casual and chatty, talking about the pandemic, sharing a funny story about teaching her fourth-grade students on Zoom, discussing her plans to adopt a dog. We rarely delved into the drama unfolding in my life, but her calls were comforting in a different way than Anna's. I knew, even in her breeziness, that she was checking on me, trying to make me feel less alone, less scared.

Maria, my Swedish friend, was there at night, at every hour. We communicated by text, a format we both preferred. I think she must have slept with her phone in her bed, with alerts on, so she could text me back right away. Those were the darkest moments, at night. There were times when I thought I could not make it to the morning, the pain was so intense.

My stepmother, Susan, called me several times a day. We were very close, bonded from the moment she entered my life in 1972. She wept with me, both of us quiet as we cried. She was the only person who tried to reach James. She emailed him in the second week, writing that in her forty-five years of practice as a family therapist, she had never seen someone leave a marriage so cruelly. She begged him to speak to me, to do therapy with me, to try to end the marriage kindly, honorably. He was furious. He texted me that, because of what Susan had written, he was going to continue his affair. He texted me that because of what she had written, he would give me nothing at all.

———

April on Martha's Vineyard feels like a snowless February. The light is flat and the temperatures stay low, the wind brisk. It rains a lot. Flowers and trees don't bloom until May.

Easter was late that year, exactly three weeks after James left us. I made cinnamon rolls, a laborious recipe requiring the dough to rise twice, and they came out of the oven as hard as hockey pucks. I trudged around the woods hiding plastic eggs with clues inside, a treasure hunt for the girls, a family tradition since I was a child. I wore a dress, trying to appear festive, and boots to manage the muddy areas. An hour into the effort, I realized I had messed up one of the connections between clues and had to redo the hunt, starting from the beginning. I felt desperate in this moment, like I had reached the point when I would break into pieces, a sad middle-aged woman in a dress and boots, disintegrating into the lake.

But as I moved toward the osprey pole, planning to hide an egg at its base, I saw wings rise and a head appear. And then another head. They were back. I thought, *I need to tell James. He will be so happy.* And then I remembered he was gone.

———

By late April, I knew I could not keep hiding the truth from the kids. I texted James that it was time to tell them and that we needed to do it together. We hadn't spoken in several weeks. He said he thought it would be better if I told them alone.

Initially, I agreed with him. I was afraid that he would expose us to COVID. He was not in quarantine; he was having an affair in the middle of New York City. We decided we would do a family Zoom call to break the news.

James's boss texted me the next day. He was a kind man, and a friend to both of us. He wrote that he understood why I was angry, but I needed to allow James to be there to tell our kids. He spoke from experience, having been divorced, having broken the news to children himself. He wrote that he was giving James his seaplane and pilot to fly to the Vineyard.

I tried to defend myself, explaining that James did not want to come, that he didn't want custody, that he was having an affair, that he was unrecognizable to me, that it was dangerous to have him appear in our house. But as my text bubbles appeared, as I reread each note, I could see how I might be perceived—a bitter woman lashing out against the man who had left her. And potentially jeopardizing James's job, his livelihood. I needed to be calm. I needed to be accommodating. I needed to shut up. And he was right—James should be there, in person, to tell the girls.

I thanked him for giving James the plane.

James met the pilot at an airport in Connecticut. Before he boarded, we called Finn together. James told him that we were divorcing. Finn was quiet. James and I kept talking, alternating back and forth, trying to assure our son that everything would be okay. For several minutes, we didn't realize that Finn had hung up, maybe as soon as he heard the headline.

I called the parents he was staying with, asking them to go look for him. I imagined him running across an open field, trying to flee the terrible news, but they found him in their basement, surrounded by his friends. The father said, "Don't worry. We've got him."

James landed on the Vineyard just before 2 p.m. He drove down our driveway in a Jeep our caretaker had left for him at the airport, a model similar to the one he'd driven onto the ferry a month earlier. He walked up the brick path to our door. He wore a mask, so I couldn't see his whole face, but my first thought was that he seemed happy, his step brisk and optimistic. He was carrying an empty duffel bag over his shoulder.

He said he had only ninety minutes until he had to return to the airport. We gathered in the living room, on the side we rarely used, where two white couches flanked a large coffee table. I sat between the girls on one of the couches, my arms around both of their small shoulders. James paced back and forth in front of us, still masked, the glass doors of our living room and the expanse of the lake behind him. He said, "Mom and I are separated and we're going to divorce. I haven't been happy."

He continued to pace while he spoke, not looking at either of the girls, not looking at me. I watched him, thinking, *The way he is moving and talking is so different. I don't recognize his body, his voice. Is he having a breakdown? Is he in love? Is he just delighted to be free of me, of us?*

As soon as he said the word *divorced,* Carrie twisted her body to face the back of the couch. She was smiling; she thought he was joking. Then she looked at me, saw my grave expression, and shrieked. I tried to grab her, but she fled down the stairs, wailing in agony.

Evie sat still and silent, with her arms crossed.

James turned to me and said, "I'm starving, can you make me a sandwich?"

I stared back at him, shocked. I didn't know what to say in front of Evie. I tried to reason out an answer, *Wouldn't a good mother make their child's father a sandwich? Wasn't this how the world said you were supposed to behave in a divorce? Be nice to each other in front of the kids?*

I said, "Okay, but please go find Carrie."

I went to the kitchen. With my hands shaking, I toasted slices of sourdough bread, spread mustard, layered turkey, sliced avocado and tomato, sprinkled sea salt. I thought, *If I'm doing this, I'm going to do it well. I will not make a shitty sandwich.* Maybe part of me thought that it would make him regret what he was doing. *How could he leave a wife who made such good sandwiches?* I thought this even though, in that moment, I didn't want him—this version of him—to stay.

I put the sandwich on a white plate with a bamboo rim and sliced it in half. I looked at our collection of cotton napkins and selected one in a blue flowered print. I roamed the house looking for him, carrying the plate and the napkin. He wasn't with either girl. Carrie was in the guest room, curled on the couch. Evie was in her bed, the covers pulled up, looking at her phone. Evie told me later that before she'd gone to her room, James had taken her out to the lawn with one of his slingshots, explaining that it was now her job to keep the geese away. He showed her how to insert the pellet, pull back the sling, aim, and shoot.

I finally found him in the basement. He had several cardboard boxes at his feet. He was squatting in front of them, rummaging through the contents—papers and folders and notebooks. I watched as he pulled down two more boxes. He was sweating with the effort. I asked him what he was doing. He turned to me with the same cold green eyes I'd seen the day he left.

He said, "I'm looking for our prenup. If you have it, you have to give it to me."

The prenup was missing. My lawyer from 1999 had died, and his firm had no record of the document. James couldn't reach his lawyer, now retired. And neither of us had a signed copy in our email.

I stood there, at the top of the basement stairs, holding the plate, watching him. I told him to stop, to be with the girls during his remaining minutes in the house, but he continued, pulling box after box off the shelves. His duffel sat open on the floor beside the boxes, ready to receive what he found.

He finally gave up his search when it was time to go back to the airport. He ate the sandwich quickly as he stood by the front door. I told the girls to come say goodbye. They leaned against the banister, staring at him.

He said, "The ospreys are back."

I nodded. "Yes, we've seen them."

When he walked to the borrowed Jeep, the girls and I got in our Toyota, a big family car, to pick up Chinese takeout from one of the only restaurants open on the island. I wanted to leave first, before James. I didn't want my daughters to see their father drive away, his car disappearing over the hill. I feared the image would stay in their minds forever. I should have known it was the image of him pacing in his mask, not looking at them as he delivered the awful news, that would stick.

The girls and I ate together at the kitchen table, watching *Gilmore Girls* as we did each night. We'd seen every episode multiple times, and the familiarity was soothing. My phone pinged. It was a text from James: "That was a great visit!"

I stared at the sentence, stunned. He had rewritten the wrenching scenes we'd just lived, making them something different, something happy.

I didn't write back.

A few weeks later, he sent an email with no message, only an attachment. It was a scan of the prenup. His lawyer had located it in a storage facility. When I opened the document and scrolled to the last page, I stopped at the sight of my own name. My signature looked innocent and hopeful, in blue ink and careful script, dated five days before our wedding.

Part II

Male ospreys court their mates. They identify a breeding area, an ideal location for a nest, and then practice a series of aerial maneuvers. When a female appears, the male performs his routine: He flies above her, often as high as three hundred feet, pauses, fans his tail feathers, and dives down again, toward the water, toward her. He usually carries something in his talons, a fish or something to build a nest—sticks, bark, grass, seaweed. The male calls for the female as he flies, a sound like a whistle of a teakettle. This courting is called a "sky-dance."

Once they reproduce, the couple is usually monogamous. They mate for several years, often for the rest of their lives.

———

James and I met in 1998 at Davis Polk, a large corporate law firm in Midtown Manhattan. The firm occupied multiple floors of a skyscraper above what used to be the Grand Central Post Office. It was modern and luxurious, all blond wood and glass, with sweeping views of the city from every office.

It was a place I never should have been. In high school, I

wanted to be a writer. I discovered writing in my first year and won several prizes for fiction before I graduated. When I arrived at college, I applied to a selective writing seminar. After submitting a sample of my work, I was admitted to the class, one of only two freshmen. I shared my first short story in October. It was about a family spending the day on the beach. I can't remember much more than that. What I do remember is a senior telling the class that it was terrible, that I couldn't write. His name was Greg. He was tall, white, and very punk rock—short, spiky blond hair, a torn concert T-shirt, big black combat boots, a leather jacket. His analysis included nothing specific about my story. It was a blanket judgment about quality and talent. The teacher, another man, said nothing. After a few minutes of tense silence, a female student rose to my defense. But it was too late. I had taken Greg's assessment as the truth, storing it in every cell of my body.

I changed my focus to public service, and I was frenetic about it. I volunteered in a nursing home, as a Big Sister, and a GED tutor. I manned a legal services hotline at Boston City Hall. It was as if I were trying to beat the writing dream out of me, drown it in altruistic purposefulness. I graduated, did a fellowship in New York City government, and went to law school.

I spent the summer after my first year of law school at the Criminal Defense Division of Legal Aid in Brooklyn, a gritty place with lawyers sitting wherever they could find a free desk. Even as an intern, I was able to be "second seat" in a trial, assisting a lawyer in a grand larceny case—the robbery of a deli—which ended in an acquittal. I did more defense work during my third year in law school, representing a twelve-year-old boy in family court, defending him against a charge of climbing into his neighbor's window to steal her shampoo (he was given probation). I loved being in a court-room. I didn't feel shy there; I could prepare almost every part of it—the direct, the cross, the closing statement—the map of it becoming clear in my mind: how to present a case, how to take a witness where I wanted them to go.

During the spring of my second year of law school, a swarm of elite law firms came to campus to hold interviews for summer associate positions. We put on suits, met with partners, and compared our "callbacks"—invitations to visit the firms for more interviews. I was swept up in all of it, the sophistication and achievement of it, the courting. I collected a dozen offers and chose Davis Polk for its reputation and, if I'm honest, its sleek and glamorous interiors. My father was surprised I didn't pick Cravath, the most prestigious of New York law firms at the time, but their offices weren't nearly as nice.

Davis Polk continued to seduce us all summer long. Our workloads were light. We were invited to lunches at the grand restaurants of the era—Bouley, Vong, Montrachet. They threw us lavish parties at the Central Park Zoo and the Empire State Building. I worked in the litigation department and, in early July, was placed on the defense team for a well-known tobacco company. I spent two weeks in a window-less conference room at their headquarters in Kansas City, reviewing binder after binder of board minutes, a painfully boring task, which also felt morally compromising. Still, there was glamour to it—defending a famous company, searching for incriminating evidence, working on a team with the best minds at the firm, including a future US senator.

At the end of the summer, Davis Polk offered me a permanent position, pending my graduation from law school and passing the bar exam. I wavered. I was still drawn to the prestige, to the idea of a few years at the firm serving as a legal finishing school, but I knew my true interest was in criminal defense. I like to think I would have chosen the public sector had my life remained stable, had everything not fallen apart.

———

On January 22, 1996, during my third year of law school, after a long group study session in my apartment in the West Village, I went to bed late. Eager for sleep, I shut off my phone's ringer. I turned my answering machine's volume down to zero.

At 8 a.m., I woke to the sound of the building intercom's buzzing. I walked the few steps from my bed to my small galley kitchen, feeling cold and confused by the sound.

I picked up the handset. The doorman said, "Your aunt is trying to reach you. She says it's an emergency."

I turned to look at the answering machine in my living room. It was blinking frantically, the number fourteen flashing. I hung up the handset, walked to the machine, and pressed play, still half asleep. The first five messages were from Susan, using my childhood nickname: "Flo, call me, it's urgent. Flo, where are you, please call." And then a series from my aunt, my father's older sister. Then several hang-ups.

I called the number at my father and Susan's apartment uptown. My aunt answered. I said, "What happened, what's wrong?"

She said, "Just come right away."

"Tell me now, what happened?"

My aunt was a loving person, but always blunt. She said, "He's dead. Your father is dead."

I called my mother. She answered. I began to sob.

She tried to calm me down, trying to find out what had happened. She asked, her voice rising, "Is it your brother?"

I said, "No. It's Pa. He died."

She said, "I'm coming."

She arrived in her station wagon thirty minutes later, still in her flowered bathrobe, and drove me up Madison Avenue, leaving me at the awning of my father and Susan's building on East 83rd Street. The doorman took me up to their apartment in the service elevator; I can't remember why. I had thrown on jeans, sneakers, and a sweater, which now felt hot, itchy. I pulled at the neck. It was normal weather for January, in the thirties, but it felt much warmer. The air in the elevator was still, stifling.

In the apartment, there were at least a dozen people milling around—several of my cousins, an old college friend of my father's, my brother and his wife, Charmaine. They had all picked up their phones, they had all answered when Susan and my aunt called, while I was still asleep. I stood in the entryway, waiting for someone to notice me.

My father and Susan's housekeeper grabbed me. She said, "You should see him before they take him away."

Before I could refuse, she pulled me down the hallway

by my wrist, to the door of my father and Susan's bedroom. He was lying in bed, on his back. His shoulders, above the sheets, were bare.

I learned later that his body had been on the ground, moved by the paramedics so they could work on him on a hard surface, and then, after they declared him dead, placed him back in bed, the covers pulled up, his eyelids closed. I wished that someone had dressed him. He looked so vulnerable.

Standing in the doorway, I could not process what had happened. My father was fifty-four and looked even younger, like the California boy he was—tall, fit, tanned, a full head of blond hair. It did not seem possible that he could die, that I could never see him again.

———

My father was a magnetic, larger-than-life figure, the center around which Susan, my brother, and I orbited. He was born and raised in Beverly Hills, his father a photographer and movie producer, his mother a silent-film actress. He was a diligent student, an altar boy, and a devoted son who, as a teenager, wrote long letters to his parents every week from his Catholic boarding school in Rhode Island. He met my mother, Amanda, when they were both in college, he a senior at Harvard and she a freshman at Wellesley. They fell swiftly in love and married in Roslyn, New York, in 1964. It was a large and lavish wedding, with trumpets, twelve bridesmaids, and nineteen ushers. She was twenty and he was twenty-three.

Their marriage made headlines because both their families had bold names, signals of American wealth and privilege. My mother's ancestors include John Jay, the first chief justice of the Supreme Court, and Henry Morgan Tilford, a founder of Standard Oil; my father was descended from the Vanderbilts. My mother's mother was Babe Paley, a fashion icon of that era and the wife of Bill Paley, the founder of CBS. As newlyweds, my parents lived a glamorous life. They had a grand apartment in the Dakota, hosted and attended notable parties, and made regular appearances in gossip columns, on best-dressed lists, and in *Vogue* magazine. My mother was famously beautiful with dark brown hair and almond-shaped hazel eyes. She was photographed by Richard Avedon and Irving Penn; my father was drawn by Andy Warhol. They were called the "It Couple," the "Fun Couple," the "Young Locomotives," and, in one fictionalized account, the "Moonflower Couple," the moonflower symbolic of beauty and romance.

My father went to law school, worked for Robert F. Kennedy as a legislative assistant, and, after Kennedy's assassination, ran for a position in the New York City Council, becoming, at that time, the youngest person ever elected to a seat. He was politically progressive, cofounding the New Democratic Coalition and drafting one of the country's first gay rights bills. The same year he was elected, at age twenty-eight, he bought a controlling interest in *The Village Voice,* beginning a lifelong interest in media, later merging the *Voice* with *New York* magazine and selling his stake to Rupert Murdoch (a decision he eventually regretted).

My brother was born in 1967, named Shirley Carter after my father and grandfather, and I was born in 1969, named Flobelle after my father's mother, the stage name she had created from her given name (Florence Belle). Flobelle died four months before I was born. At her funeral, my father concluded his eulogy by announcing that if I was a girl, I would be named for her. He had not discussed it with my pregnant mother who sat, stunned, in the front pew. She decided I would go by Belle, her small rebellion.

My parents loved each other but they were too young, too immature, to make the marriage work. They fought a lot, both had affairs, and divorced in 1972, when I was still two. By the terms of their joint-custody agreement, typical at that time, my brother and I saw our father only every other weekend, on alternating holidays, and for a few weeks in the summer. He was not a hands-on father, but he enjoyed us and wanted more time with us. He dreaded Sunday nights, the moment we left him, when we were taken back to our mother's apartment.

My father met Susan shortly after he and my mother divorced. Susan was twenty-three and dazzling in a different way than my mother—six feet tall with long, thick blond hair and blue eyes, a social worker and former homecoming queen, born on Long Island and raised in Ohio. She turned my father down at first, disliking his reputation as a socialite, but finally agreed to an early dinner at the Ginger Man on the Upper West Side. Within an hour, they both knew they would spend the rest of their lives together, the attraction and chemistry between them instant. They discovered they had the same favorite book, *The Brothers Karamazov,* and they walked through Central Park after dinner, to the Doubleday Book Shop on Fifth Avenue, so my father could buy her his favorite anthology of poetry. They were joined that night,

threaded together in both intellect and heart, and they never
again parted.

My brother and I loved Susan immediately. She was
young and fun and gathered us up, spending hours making
sandcastles with my brother on the beach in East Hampton,
dining on soups of toilet paper at my pretend restaurants,
reading to us at bedtime. The weekends my father had custody, she picked me up at school on Friday and took me to
buy a bologna sandwich wrapped in white paper from a deli
on Madison Avenue, or if my father was with us, to Melon's
for a bacon cheeseburger and cottage fries. Susan and my
father married in our living room in 1977 and brought me
and my brother on their honeymoon to La Samanna, a new
beachfront hotel in St. Martin, a place we returned to every
spring for almost twenty years.

My father and Susan were, to me, the perfect couple, my
example of a great marriage. When I think of them, I see
them dancing together in our kitchen, the same height, their
long legs in blue jeans, their arms around each other. My
father was the flower, needy of attention, and Susan was the
gardener, a natural caretaker, and that dynamic worked for
them. They experienced the world with a similar lustful cu-
riosity and sense of fun. They conducted Beethoven's Ninth
Symphony in bed together every New Year's Eve. They
drank red wine and played chess late into the night. They
hosted friends for lively dinners and long weekends at their
house in Water Mill on Long Island. They were adored for
being genuine and relaxed, never pretentious. They loved
dogs, especially pugs, a passion my father acquired from my
mother. At one point, they had five of them, four fawn and

one black, all named after members of the family, all allowed to sleep on their bed, a chorus of snoring.

My father was an intellectual, reading several books a week, mostly history and biographies, but he loved less erudite culture too—he had more than a dozen magazines delivered from a newsstand every Monday, a stack we could not touch until he had read them all. He was a great writer, always composing on large yellow legal pads with black felt-tip pens, in a distinct, nearly illegible scrawl. He wrote an adventure tale on one of those pads for me and my brother, reading installments to us on Saturday nights in his study as we drank mugs of warm milk mixed with honey.

He had an extraordinary eye as a collector. In the 1960s and '70s, he bought paintings by Jasper Johns, Frank Stella, and Mark Rothko, among others, a collection he sold in the 1980s to finance his real passion, first editions of twentieth-century American literature (an epically unwise trade; many of those paintings are worth millions of dollars today). My father and Susan's apartments, at the River House on East 52nd Street, and later on Fifth Avenue, and their house in Water Mill, were filled with all his collections, including drawings, wooden staircases, bronze sculptures, and hundreds of pieces of treen—voting boxes, perfume bottles, miniature shoes. Almost every room had shelves filled with his books, the regular ones next to the collectible first editions, the latter in custom-made black, red, or brown boxes. My middle-school years were filled with the sounds of him opening boxes of books and cutting reams of clear plastic to cover them. I had to angle myself slightly to get to my bedroom because he had installed bookcases on both sides of the narrow hallway.

My father was handsome, always carrying the air of the California boy he had been, but perfectly dressed in an East Coast way, in Savile Row suits, Turnbull & Asser shirts, and John Lobb shoes when formal; jeans, long-sleeved polo shirts, and driving shoes from Hunting World on the weekends. He smoked a pipe at all hours of the day and carried leather pouches of Dunhill tobacco in his jacket pockets. He loved food, both fine dining and junk, equally passionate about the French restaurant Lutèce and Big Macs (he could eat two in one sitting). He loved to travel and packed meticulously for every trip, filling large black Hermès suitcases with his clothes and a portable stereo to play classical music. He wore a "man purse" (Hermès too), slung across his torso to hold his wallet and traveler's checks. He loved shopping of all kinds. He was generous and spoiling. He never let anyone else pick up a check. He was charming and funny and often outrageous, swearing without hesitation, saying inappropriate things. But he was also introverted. He always preferred to stay home over going out, and he hated the phone. We were most similar in this, in our shyness, our introversion.

My father was not always easy. He was moody and had a temper, occasionally a scary one, but usually more like a child who needed to be managed. He yelled and stomped his feet—literally—when he didn't get his way. When he napped on weekend afternoons, we had to stay completely quiet, moving carefully around him, anticipating a period of intense grumpiness when he woke up. My brother also had a temper, and my father said his mother did too; it was accepted as a Burden family trait. Susan could manage him and my brother; she didn't wilt or retreat, but also allowed it to go on. In this environment, I became even quieter, more cautious, watchful.

My father and I were close in many ways. We had inside jokes. Every time we were in a car, from childhood well into adulthood, I would ask him, "Where are we going?" and he would answer "Puerto Rico." I can't remember why. He wrote me letters in the voice of each pug when I was at sleepaway camp. And we bonded over collecting. I had my own, less expensive collections—stacks of Dannon yogurt tops foraged in my grade-school cafeteria, puffy stickers placed in photo albums, porcelain figurines, and, most passionately, *Archie* comic books. When I was little, he bought me all the latest issues—*Archie, Jughead, Betty & Veronica*— from a small comic store on Second Avenue and showed me how to create a catalog, which I typed onto thin onionskin pages. On my twenty-first birthday, he gave me *Archie* No. 1, from 1942, placed in a custom black box, the name and date in gold on the spine.

My father was proud of me, of my studiousness, of my decision to become a lawyer, following his example; he told me this often. But when he died, we were still parent and child, shy people who had not yet broken through. As I stood in his doorway, looking at his profile, his skin beginning to drain of color, I was not yet conscious of all that he would miss—weddings, grandchildren, growing old with Susan. All I could feel was the horror of death, the shock of it, the sensation of being completely unprepared.

———

In my father and Susan's bedroom, their housekeeper said, "You should kiss him goodbye." She and I were both Catholic, as was my father. It was what one was supposed to do. But I couldn't bring myself to move closer to him. I shook my head and left the room.

I found Susan in the kitchen. We held each other, crying. My brother put his arms around us.

Susan told us she had taken their two dogs out at 6:30 that morning. She asked my father what time he wanted to get up. He said 7 a.m. She set the alarm clock for him and left. When she returned, the elevator door opening directly into the apartment, she heard the clock's beeping, loud and steady, coming from their bedroom down the hall.

She said, her voice shaking, "As soon as I heard it, I knew he was dead."

For several weeks after my father's death, after his funeral at St. Ignatius Loyola on Park Avenue, after his burial next to his parents at Woodlawn Cemetery in the Bronx, in the middle of the night I would panic, believing he was not really dead, that we had buried him alive. I would wake Susan up and beg her to intervene, to dig him up, to save him.

———

The cause of my father's death, the phrase listed on his death certificate, was "sudden arrhythmia death syndrome," defined as a fatal heart attack in a victim who is young and seems to be in good health. He had known for decades that he had a heart defect; his aortic valve was damaged and leaked, the result, perhaps, of a bout with scarlet fever as a child. He knew he would need surgery at some point to replace the valve. He had checkups with a cardiologist every six months. The last appointment had been only two months before his death, and the results were good. The doctor told him he could postpone surgery another year.

I had gone to that final appointment with my father and Susan. When he completed his tests, he walked down the hallway in his hospital gown, his fists raised in triumph, knowing he had avoided surgery again. He dreaded the idea of being cut open, his chest scarred, months of recovery. He wanted to delay it as long as he could.

After getting dressed, he sat with us in his doctor's office. The doctor asked, "What medications do you take at home?"

My father pulled out a list he'd compiled on one of his yellow legal notepads, using his felt-tip black pen, in his unique scrawl. He read it out loud: "Advil, Anacin, Afrin, Prozac. Occasionally, when I can't sleep, Ambien."

The doctor nodded and said, "Okay, none of that concerns me."

Two months after his death, we learned that he had omitted a prescription diet drug from his list. My father had a long history with diet drugs. His mother, the former actress, gave him and his sister diet pills in their teens. In college, he started taking thyroid medication to speed up his metabolism. He took it on and off through his twenties and thirties. During this time, in photographs lovingly taped in our leather family photo albums by Susan, he appears gaunt and bug-eyed.

When he died, my brother, Susan, and I believed he hadn't

taken diet drugs in a decade. He loved food but was equally obsessed with health, walking miles in Central Park every day, doing yoga, hiking in Arizona several times a year. He looked healthy and trim but not too thin, no bug eyes, not as many mood swings. And there he was in the cardiologist's office reciting his list of medications. All prescribed or over-the-counter. All innocent.

Nothing showed up in his autopsy, performed two days after he died. We spent a month thinking how tragically un-lucky he was, in the mere two percent rate of sudden death associated with his condition, a much lower risk than dying during valve replacement surgery. But then the confession came, his assistant telling Susan that she had been making him appointments with a diet doctor for the last year. He had opened a new account at Zitomer Pharmacy on Madi-son Avenue, picking up his prescribed pills in person, hiding the amber plastic bottles from Susan. We don't think the diet drug killed him—he probably would have died anyway—but it could have had an impact. We buried the secret, omit-ting this detail from the story of his death. We felt ashamed of it somehow, and protective of him; we wanted his life story to be pristine.

For Susan, the secret felt like a deep betrayal, as shock-ing as an affair. She started having dreams about him, dreams she still has today, where he appears as a stranger, cold and remote, alive but married to a different woman, with a dif-ferent family. When she wakes up, she pushes this shadow away, reminding herself that their intimacy, their bond, was real, that his secret is revealing only of his frailty, his demons.

There was another revelation that came soon after my

father died, another blow that forever altered my understanding of him. My father left an estate that was forty mil-
lion dollars in debt, carrying both personal loans and loans
to his media company, one from a bank and one from our
extended-family investment partnership, a group that included my aunt and my Burden cousins. It is not unusual
to take on this kind of debt when growing a business, but
my father's collateral was his and Susan's apartment, their
house, and their collections, so it was possible they could
have lost everything if the lenders had called the loans.
Susan knew this was the state of things, a life on the edge
of potential ruin, and they didn't hide it from me and my
brother. They even made jokes about the loans, about the
bank owning their apartment, but we didn't understand the
scope of it until he died. He had spent money like he had an
endless supply, and we'd believed that it was exactly that—
endless.

———

I returned to Davis Polk as an associate in September 1996,
eight months after my father's death. It felt like the adult
choice—a job with a significant salary, one that would cover
my rent, a career step that would have impressed my father.
I moved from the litigation department to the corporate department, a change that made no sense: Corporate work had
no research, writing, or court time—the parts of the law I
enjoyed—and I had no interest in finance. I could not even
read a balance sheet. But I didn't want to be placed back on
the tobacco company defense team. I had chosen the private
sector, but I felt like I had to draw a line somewhere. I could

have asked the assigning partners to move me to a new case; they would have done it. But it felt easier, less confrontational, to just switch departments.

Corporate was divided into three groups—banking, mergers and acquisitions, and securities—and the firm's clients were some of the biggest banks and companies in the world. I started in banking and was quickly claimed by a gruff male partner who terrified me. With almost no training, I drafted and negotiated debt provisions with banks and opposing counsels, pretending I understood what they meant, faking my way through it. In my second year, I rotated from banking to securities, spending nights at the printer, traveling around the country to do due diligence. I worked hard and I figured out how to do the job, but I hated it—the punishing hours, the demanding clients, the phone calls that came just as I was putting on my coat on a Friday evening, knowing, as I saw the partner's name appear on the screen, that I would be there all night, all weekend. I cried in the bathroom almost every day.

I was managing more than the demands of the job. Susan, my brother, and I met with lawyers and financial advisers every week, sometimes every day, to sort out my father's estate and sell his company. The sale allowed us to repay his loans and regain some wealth, in part because of Susan's status as a widow, which exempted her from paying capital-gains taxes. But the stress continued. Two years after my father's death, I was still fielding calls from lawyers and bankers, still having heated arguments with my brother and Susan about investments and expenses. I took these calls in a small telephone booth in the Davis Polk offices, trying to keep this part of my life hidden from other associates, ashamed of the mess we were in.

Every phone call filled me with dread. The conversations, the decisions, the arguments were intertwined with the shock and grief of my father's death, a pervasive and unrelenting sense of doom. It matched my unhappiness at the firm. I felt pressure and fear wherever I turned.

———

Another associate, a friend, introduced me to James in March of 1998. James was in his fifth year at the firm, recently returned from a six-month stint in the Hong Kong office. I'd seen him before, passing each other in the wide, carpeted hallways, nodding politely, but we'd never met.

When my friend brought me into James's office, I was carrying an Academy Awards ballot. My family had an Oscar pool, a tradition since I was little, and I was considering my choices. James sat at his desk, my friend and I sat in two chairs facing him.

I said, "What do you guys think? Who for Best Actress?" I listed the names, including Judi Dench and Kate Winslet.

James looked confused. He said, "I've never heard of them."

I said, "What about Best Picture? Did you see *Good Will Hunting*?"

He said, "No, I don't know what that is. I saw *Titanic*. Is that on the list?"

I thought, *Who is this guy?*

I found him handsome, but I was not interested. In addition to his lack of movie knowledge, I could tell he was a typical New York private-school kid, the boarding-school and Ivy League variety, just like me. And he looked like my father—blond, six-foot-one, lean, with proper shoes, his shirtsleeves rolled up. It was too familiar, the WASP-y preppiness, too appropriate.

My boyfriend at the time was unemployed. He'd lost his job at a news program within days of moving in with me, a decision he pressured me into right after my father's death, when I left the West Village for an apartment on East 85th Street. I was too shell-shocked to refuse him. As I discussed the ballot with James, my boyfriend was probably sitting on my couch, watching CNBC, his feet on my antique coffee table, still sweaty from the gym. He couldn't pay any of our rent.

A month after the Oscar discussion in James's office, I was rotated into his group, Investment Management. My new office was three doors down from his and I was soon assigned to a deal he was running, the IPO of an internet holding company. As we worked together, I was impressed. He was very smart. He could parse and fix a memo or prospectus flawlessly within an hour; his markup looked like a work of art. He was quietly confident and always polite. He was adored by his clients and his assistant, an older woman from Long Island, the wife of a firefighter. We often sat side by side, working on a document. Once, our hands, holding pencils, brushed against each other (he was left-handed; I was right-handed). To my surprise, I felt a jolt, a spark.

While James looked like my father, there were important differences. Unlike my father's unusual path through politics and media, James, as a senior associate at the firm, had a traditional job, going to work each morning in his suit, taking business trips, like a dependable father in a television show. He was ambitious about a career and making a living in a way my father, as someone with inherited money, never was. And James was calm and even-tempered, never moody. His voice was always gentle. If you had asked me to describe him then, I would have used the word *steady*.

He had a girlfriend and broke up with her sometime that spring, I can't remember when, but I noted it. On my birthday in May, he offered to write a complicated memo assigned to me by a partner. He stayed late into the night to do it so that I could go out to dinner with my family and friends.

A few weeks later, he came into my office and showed me a card he'd received in the mail from the Morgan Library. It was an announcement of a talk I was giving to a group of young members about my father's book collection, which we'd just donated to the library. James, holding the card aloft, looked shocked.

He said, "This is you?"

I felt embarrassed, like I'd been found out, but I was also happy, relieved, that he had discovered the other side of my life.

He came to the lecture, sitting in the back of the audience with his roommate, Mark. He brought me a Coke at the reception, weaving around my boyfriend. My brother asked, "Who's the blond?"

In June, he sent me an email with the subject line "Going off the record here." It was the dawn of email; any message was exciting, but this one seemed to glow in my inbox. It read, "Would you be interested in ditching your boyfriend and coming to Greece with me this August?"

I waited until the next morning to answer, something rambling about liking to spend time with him, but no, I could not go. I had received a notice from my landlord that she was selling our apartment and that we needed to move out by the end of the month. I told my boyfriend I did not want to move into a new apartment together, but I was not yet brave enough to break off the relationship completely.

I'd only had three serious boyfriends in my life, and each relationship lasted for years. I didn't have casual encounters and never flirted—I was too shy, too lacking in confidence. I needed men to pursue me, to be serious and certain. And when the relationship had run its course, I was always too afraid to break it off. The prospect of hurting someone's feelings paralyzed me. I had been in love with my college boyfriends but never with this one. He had somehow ended up there, in my life, on my couch, and I didn't know how to get myself out of it.

———

On June 26, I worked late into the night preparing to leave for a vacation—a hiking trip with Susan, her mother, and my cousin. James walked into my office and shut the door behind him. Without thinking, I stood and stepped from behind my desk.

He said, "I just wanted to say goodbye."

He paused, several feet away from me. After a few beats of silence, we moved toward each other quickly, embracing, kissing—an equal, impassioned wanting of each other. The chemistry people talk about—pure physical chemistry—was coursing through me. Something had happened.

He put his hand on my cheek. His hand was shaking.

He said, "Have a great trip," kissed me again, and left my office. I was stunned. And electrified.

I left the next day and, according to Susan, spent the week of hiking in a daze, barely speaking. At the end of June, I moved out of my apartment on East 85th Street and into the third floor of a brownstone two blocks away, on the same block where Susan lived, where my father had died. I had the conversation with my boyfriend that I'd avoided for a year, ending the relationship. It took ten minutes.

On my first day back in the office, the first day James and I were both single, July 6, he took me to an AT&T cell phone store and bought me my first cell phone, a Nokia. It was navy blue, my favorite color. For a long time, he was the only person who had my number, the number I still have today. When it rang, my pulse raced.

With my new phone in hand, we left the office together in the late evening, when the hot July sun was cooling, and took the subway from Grand Central to Brooklyn Bridge. Before we got on, he took my hand and guided me to the downtown end of the platform, where the last car would open, so that our exit at City Hall Park would be easy. I loved this feeling, his gentle authority. As we walked north on Broadway, he pointed out the Woolworth Building, the Tweed Courthouse, the Sun Building. He talked about each building's history, the city's history, things I hadn't known.

He lived on the corner of White and Church streets, next to the Baby Doll Lounge, in a loft he shared with Mark, a friend from boarding school. Mark owned the building and James was the superintendent, his barter for rent. Tenants often called James at work, when the elevator broke down, when the heat wasn't working, when they needed an exterminator. He solved each problem—calling handymen, dispatching elevator companies, calming tempers—while he ran securities deals.

James and Mark's loft was on the fourth floor, divided in two by a heavy metal door they usually kept open. An elevator arrived at James's side; a staircase led to Mark's. James's side was monastic, only his bed, a desk, a chair. Mark's side was warm, filled with books and art and comfortable furniture, a pool table, and an open kitchen. When they met in boarding school, Mark was a star—respected as an athlete and a scholar. James was not a star; he had poor grades and often got in trouble. He'd also had several brushes with the law, first at sixteen, when he used a BB gun to shoot out the back window of an empty Mercedes in East Hampton. The owner of the Mercedes pressed charges, and James and his co-conspirator, his best friend, spent the night in a pink cell in East Hampton's jail. James told me that he was arrested again a year or so later, the first person to be charged under Massachusetts's new DUI law for mopeds.

James went to Kenyon College thinking it was Denison (he mixed them up in his mind). When he arrived in the cornfields of Ohio, he said a switch went off. He started studying, planning his escape. He transferred to Cornell and graduated summa cum laude. He went to work at the Manhattan DA's office, then to Yale Law School, then to Davis Polk.

Evidence of the bad boy remained. He had a tattoo (a Greek pottery shard) on one of his inner biceps, smoked Marlboro Reds, and kept his first mug shot on his bulletin board, a teenager in profile. He told me stories of the many women in his wake, some of them stalking him, unable to accept his rejection. This narrative was sexy to me, the former rebel dressed in a suit, the problem child landing at an elite law firm, the heartbreaker. He was the perfect combination of exciting and safe.

In adulthood, James and Mark switched roles. While James cleaned up, Mark's life became more complicated. After inheriting a fortune at twenty-one and winning acclaim as a writer of short stories, he started partying heavily. When James left the loft in the morning to go to work, Mark and his friends were often still awake, playing music and pool, drinking. Mark was delighted by James's transformation into a responsible adult. He looked to him for guidance; he depended on him for stability.

That first night in the apartment, James showed me around the empty loft, Mark's side and his, the roof, and then, finally, his bedroom.

He said, "Every single night, for the last two months, I've woken up at three a.m., thinking of you."

When I'd anticipated a physical relationship with him, I had imagined something sweet, but this was both tender and thrilling. It was a revelation. James was so confident, so in charge, but also vulnerable, shaking again, with the emotion of our coming together.

When we left the apartment to get dinner, as I saw him confidently descend the wide, steep stairs at the back of the apartment, tucking in his striped oxford shirt as he held the heavy door for me, I thought, *I am going to marry him.*

———

The rest of the summer was a blur of weekends in his bed and mine, clandestine encounters behind locked doors at the office, backgammon and gimlets in the loft with Mark, late dinners at Barocco, a restaurant a block from his apartment. He brought me to Chinatown and gave me my first soup dumpling, and to the Oyster Bar for my first oyster. He had perfect table manners and was always a gentleman, running me a bath, making me a latte, once gently ironing the skirt of my suit while I was wearing it.

After three weeks, he said, "Tell me you love me." I did.

When we had dinner with my brother and Charmaine at The Odeon, introducing them for the first time, I felt so proud, watching them talk as I held James's hand under the table. I'd always envied my brother and Charmaine's relationship, their passionate love for each other, and now I had it too. After dinner, my brother said, "My sister has grown up."

I brought James to Balthazar to meet my mother, to Water Mill to meet Susan. We were all over each other, kissing at meals, unrestrained in our desire for each other. My family was stunned—by the speed of it, to see me so enamored— but they were happy too, glad that I had found someone I loved so much.

I went to Greece, accepting the invitation James had extended in that first glowing email. I loved traveling with him. He took care of everything, making hotel reservations, both expensive and dirt cheap, finding great restaurants, bringing me an ice-cold cocktail while I showered. We started in Athens, then Ios, and finally Palaikastro, a small town on the Eastern end of Crete, for his stepfather's seventieth birthday party. His stepfather was an archaeologist for half the year, running a dig in Palaikastro, and a boarding-school teacher the other half. For decades, he'd brought students to work on the site in the summer. James spoke with reverence about being one of those students, spending high-school and college summers on the dig, working long hours, unearthing relics, recording his findings, his hair turning nearly white in the sun. The tattoo on his inner biceps, the pottery shard, was an homage to their work, to the precious things they had found.

We stayed at a hotel on a cliff that cost ten dollars a night, where the August winds woke us up early. We ate Greek yogurt with thick local honey and rich black coffee for breakfast and went to topless beaches where James covered me with the island's famous mud. His stepfather's birthday party was at a taverna in the small village. James knew all the locals and spoke to them in nearly fluent Greek. We drank raki, ate platters of freshly caught fish and perfectly grilled lamb chops, and sang "Happy Birthday" in Greek. We could not keep our hands off each other.

On a ferry from Crete back to Athens, we lay on the floor, our heads on our duffel bags. James asked me if I wanted to have children. I said I did. He said, "We're going to get married. We're going to have a family together."

In September, we went to City Hall and got a marriage license, a requirement in New York before getting married. We didn't tell anyone about it. It wasn't an engagement, but it was a private declaration of our love, of our intent. We made photocopies of the thin paper and kept them in our desks.

In October, James went to Asia on a long-planned trip with Mark. Since email was still dial-up and neither of us had laptops, we sent each other faxes, using the Davis Polk fax form. I still have all of them, the faxes and our emails, clipped together, protected like heirlooms in a cabinet in my apartment. The exchanges are charming and clever, filled with love and lust, of longing for each other. We also kept a diary together, a small red one with thin blue pages. We took turns filling in the days with a mechanical pencil, recording everything we did together, handing it back and forth, delighting each other with the words we chose, the way we crafted short sentences, making the most of the narrow space allotted for each date.

Every day, every interaction, felt romantic and passionate. Even when I saw his name appear on the display of my work phone, the neat five letters of his first and last names flashing, I was flooded with something—a sense of destiny, security, love. But it was more than that. It was intimate. I felt known. He understood my heartbreak and confusion over my father's death, the ups and downs of my friendships, the details of my calls in the phone booth, the hundreds of *Archie* comic books in my closet. I knew the details of his life too, the things he loved, the arc of his journey from fuckup to star lawyer, his romances and his adventures, his love and worry for Mark. We told each other things late at night and early in the morning, on the subway to work, whispering in each other's ears, confiding again and again, in person and on the page.

———

James's most tender topic was his family. Each word, as it came from his mouth, seemed to hurt him. He told me his parents had both grown up with money, in nice apartments in Manhattan, attending private schools and impressive colleges. But at some point in the 1970s, his father had a breakdown, was laid off, and stopped working. As the years went by, his parents had to spend their savings to cover basic living expenses and school tuition. They lived in a classic seven-room prewar apartment on East 74th Street, next to the all-boys' private school James and his brother attended, but signs of the unrelenting financial pressure were everywhere—holes in carpets and jeans, sneakers that were always too small, overdue bills. They never went out to dinner, never went on vacation. It was a stark contrast to James's friends, who were not just solvent, but very wealthy. James learned to get invited on trips with his classmates—spring break in the Caribbean, Christmas in Brazil, August in East Hampton—to make his life bigger, but there was a pervasive sense that it was all going to fall apart. And it did. When James was in law school, his parents divorced, sold their apartment for a fraction of its value, and revealed their empty coffers. His father moved to Norwalk, Connecticut, renting a one-room apartment in another family's house, becoming a hermit, refusing all luxuries, even a television.

There was another thread of the story, one that James wouldn't talk about, a whisper I heard over the years but could never hold on to—his father leaving the family abruptly, abandoning his life as a husband and father, maybe after an affair, but coming back, returning to East 74th Street for a period of years before James's mother filed for divorce. When I asked about it, even after many years of marriage, James would shut down, unwilling to discuss it. It was the third rail, a piece of him I could not go near.

James seemed to carry the story of his father and his family's financial ruin like a hard nut in his chest, painful and motivating at the same time. I never learned the full story, but I could feel its edges. I could see its effect: James's drive to make money, to support his parents, to protect himself from a similar fate. And to create his own family, one he could make secure. He told me how much he wanted to be a husband and father. He told me how much he wanted an honorable life.

———

When James landed at JFK after his trip with Mark, he asked me to meet him at the clock in Grand Central at noon, a short walk from our offices. I got there early, circling the information booth, running into a partner who was picking up her train schedule. I saw him descend the stairs. He was wearing a tweed jacket and had grown a beard. My breath caught. He was so handsome.

He walked over to me, grabbed me in an embrace, and whispered in my ear, "Will you marry me?"

I whispered in his, "Yes."

He reached into his jacket pocket and pulled out a sapphire ring, loose with no box, the blue stone encircled with small diamonds. He put it on my finger.

He said, "Nothing bad will ever come of this."

It was three months after our first kiss.

I felt it all: love, lust, joy, and a letting go of the anxiety, the gripping I'd felt since my father was found dead in his bed. James was here. He had arrived exactly when I needed him. It was the romance my favorite books, my favorite movies, and my family had told me to want and expect—he had swept me off my feet, quickly and completely. And, as he told me often, he was going to take care of me. The fatherless girl had found her knight.

———

The speed of our beginning and the speed of our ending, of his exit, felt like matching bookends. They both came out of nowhere. They both left me reeling. In both instances, he was definitive, certain. There was no gray area. The switch went on, and then it went off. He wanted it, he wanted me. And then he didn't.

Were there red flags? The subtle or not subtle warnings I should have seen before we married, the ones people ask me about now, wanting something—anything—to prove that our fate could have been predicted, that the same thing couldn't happen to them? Maybe the shift in personality at Kenyon. Maybe the arrests and the breaking of girls' hearts. Maybe his tendency to direct, and mine to follow. Maybe the untold tale of his father. But these felt like stories of a rebellious boy becoming a responsible man; the normal mysteries of a three-dimensional human being. There is nothing I look back on now and say, *How could I have missed that?* Other couples I knew then, and know now, had many more flags, redder flags, and they stayed married.

And doesn't it all look different, wouldn't your own story look different, if you knew how it was going to end?

———

After we left Grand Central, we told everyone we were engaged, calling our parents, our siblings, our friends. We met a large group for dinner at a restaurant in Tribeca to celebrate. We were both elated. James wanted to be married as soon as possible, but I wanted some time to plan our wedding. We settled on the first Saturday in June.

The news of our engagement spread quickly through Davis Polk. Within days, I was moved out of James's group and back to the general securities pool. Partners didn't like couples working together, even though, by some accounts, thirty percent of Davis Polk's lawyers had met their spouse at the firm. I quit four months later, in March 1999, becoming the stereotype of a woman who leaves a job as soon as she finds a husband, but I was relieved to get out of there. I went to work as general counsel of my brother's company, an internet-hosting venture he started in 1993. He needed someone to draft contracts for clients and vendors. I thought it was temporary, a way to escape Davis Polk, a brief stop on my way back to the public sector.

I had always worshipped my brother. Only nineteen

months apart, we were allies in childhood, shuttled side by side between our mother and father, sharing an understanding of the strange particularities of our parents, our homes, our nannies. We fought in all the normal ways siblings do; I can still summon the terror I felt when he chased me down hallways, the rush to lock my door before he reached me, and there were also years when he ignored me. But once I became a teenager, he adopted me again, introducing me to his friends, keenly interested in making me cool, an uphill battle with a painfully shy little sister. He took me to my first concert, The Clash, when I was thirteen. He introduced me to Tower Records, vintage Levi's, Brooks Brothers tweed overcoats. He insisted I accompany him to nightclubs—Danceteria in the Hamptons, Limelight and Area in the city—all of which I found scary, counting the minutes until I could go home. He gave me my first cocktail, a vodka tonic in St. Martin (I liked it) and my first drag of pot (I hated it). When I went to boarding school, he gave me a Frankie Goes to Hollywood poster and dozens of records—the Cure, Talking Heads, UB40— which I played loudly on my stereo in my dorm room. He explained the internet to me long before anyone had heard of it and bought me my first computer.

My brother failed to make me cool—I would never be that—but he made me a little less nerdy. When I went to work for him, it felt like where I should be in that moment: siblings joining forces in the wake of our father's death, me supporting his growing company. Our skills complemented each other—the visionary entrepreneur and the rules-oriented lawyer.

———

As soon as we were engaged, James and I moved into a rental apartment on Worth Street. It was a loft with two bedrooms and a roof deck. He created a checklist of things we needed to do to combine our lives—setting up cable TV, booking movers, ordering blackout shades. We loved crossing things off the list. It felt so grown-up. We split the rent, utilities, and other costs down the middle, starting our commitment to dividing things evenly. I picked up the check at dinner as often as he did. I felt proud of this, my ability to pay my equal share.

I filled the apartment with my things: a mahogany bed, my grandfather's desk, my father's Sally Mann photographs to hang over the white couch. James arrived with almost nothing, just his clothes and a few framed posters from the White Street loft. But we shared a similar aesthetic— minimalist, masculine, no bright colors or patterns—so it soon felt like it belonged to both of us.

A few months before our wedding, my mother reminded me that James and I had to sign a prenuptial agreement. When my brother and I were in our early twenties, we signed a contract with her, agreeing that we would have prenups when we got married. All of my assets were in trust, entirely protected in case of divorce, whether we had a prenup or not. I didn't think I needed it. But I had committed to having one.

My brother and Charmaine signed a prenup before their wedding in 1996, and our family lawyer, Tom, sent the same template to me, James, and James's lawyer two months before our wedding. The draft said that any asset we brought individually to the marriage would remain ours, not subject to division, but anything earned during the marriage, and anything in joint name, would be split if we divorced.

James was upset when I told him about the prenup. He said it made him feel like an outsider, a threat. I felt guilty asking him to sign it. The draft sat on my desk for a month, unaddressed.

A few weeks before our wedding, as I felt increasing pressure from my lawyer to get the document signed, James asked me to make one amendment to the agreement: instead of sharing anything earned during the marriage, only assets that had been put in joint name would be split. Anything that was in my name alone, or his name alone, would not be split. James explained that it was fair to do it this way, that we should each keep what we made during the marriage unless we affirmatively chose to share it. His reasoning made sense to me.

With James sitting beside me, I called Tom to request the change. I put the call on speaker phone. I did not tell Tom that James was listening. Tom told me it was a bad idea; it was standard to share in what was earned during a marriage, both by James and by me. It was what my brother and Charmaine had done, what most couples do. It was fair. I made the counterargument, repeating the words James had given to me to explain why we should make the change. Finally, Tom said, "Okay, Belle, if this is what you want."

After we hung up, I felt a wave of anxiety. I was going against legal advice. But James was my family now, my soon-to-be husband, the future father of my children, the love of my life. He was the man I trusted most. And our wedding was only three weeks away; any conflict over the prenup could derail the whole thing. I didn't tell my mother, Susan, or my brother about the change. I worried they would intervene, that they would stop me.

Tom revised the document and sent us new drafts. We signed it on May 30 and married on June 5.

———

Our wedding was at my family's house in Water Mill, a farmhouse with eight acres of land, an apple orchard, a rose garden, a tennis court, and a pool. We knew the wedding had to be small or it would balloon to hundreds of people; my mother and Susan would both have long lists. I was never someone who imagined a big wedding—the thought of all that attention made me anxious—so we decided to limit it to eighty guests, forty for each of us.

It was beautiful, more like a big dinner party than a wedding. I wore a slinky satin dress designed by Calvin Klein at my mother's request since she was friendly with him. My brother walked me down the aisle. A judge married us under an open tent facing Mecox Bay. Dinner was set up at one long table between an allée of sycamore trees. Mark circled the length of it as he gave his toast. A dozen other friends took the microphone to talk about James, about me, about us together. A small group watched a Knicks playoff game in my father's study after dinner; I threw my bouquet from the adjoining balcony after they won. James did not want dancing, and I conceded (my one regret about that day), so we set up what looked like a nightclub under lanterns by the pool, playing a mix my brother had made, hanging out, James's friends and mine, late into the night. At 3 a.m., a driver in a rented Rolls-Royce drove us back to the city and we checked into the St. Regis, the same hotel where my grandparents had an apartment in the 1960s.

We flew to Asia the next day, starting a honeymoon James had planned meticulously: a grand hotel in Bangkok, a luxury tent on a remote Indonesian island, a week on the beach in Bali, eating our way through Hong Kong. Susan warned me that a honeymoon could turn out to be disappointing, a victim of too-high expectations (she had seen this often in her practice as a family therapist). But ours was anything but. We were so in love, so attracted to each other, so excited about being married. James knew every location well, having lived in Hong Kong. His expertise made all of it feel exciting and romantic.

We had one fight, during an outdoor dinner in Bali, over my tendency to pay restaurant checks without looking at the bill, something James had witnessed in New York and made note of. He told me this would not be the way we did things in our marriage. I was surprised by his upset, by his scolding. My family never opened the padded black folder at restaurants before handing over our card; we trusted the calculation and tipped heavily. But the habit made James anxious. We were now tied to each other financially, and he worried I would be a profligate spender, like my father. I was defensive and argued the point, but his admonition also made me feel safe. He was going to make sure I never ended up in trouble.

We came home and started our married life together.

He left Davis Polk the following year and became general counsel at an investment firm founded by my uncle. He soon moved to a senior management role at the firm, abandoning his law degree. I continued to work for my brother, his legal needs increasing as his business grew. I liked the work, the combination of contract law, human resources, and the dynamics of a start-up. I had stock options and believed in the promise of the company.

I also felt stuck, not wanting to disappoint my brother by leaving. I tried to keep my own interests alive—starting a website about volunteering, taking on pro bono domestic violence cases—but it wasn't enough. I had marooned myself again, following a dream that was not my own, moving further away from the person I'd planned to be.

———

In November 1999, five months after our wedding (and six months after his own), Mark was found dead of a heroin overdose in his bathroom in the White Street loft. He had been doing well, happy to be married, preparing for the publication of his first novel, so his death was a terrible, horrifying shock. James was devastated. They were so close, so tied to each other. James felt like he had failed in his most important job: making sure Mark was okay. He had moved out of the loft less than a year earlier, consumed with our romance. They had both married. James had stopped paying attention.

Mark was also the source of all that was exciting and unpredictable in James's life. They traveled together often, to Asia and Europe, unruly adventures James loved. James also seemed to live vicariously through Mark, thrilled by his freedom and his bad behavior. Mark said what he wanted and did what he wanted, not caring who he upset or offended. He was known to be a disrupter, hurling insults, causing damage, while James walked the straight path, reporting to clients and partners, burying the wild teenager he had been.

After Mark's funeral, James said to me, "I don't have anything to look forward to anymore." I wasn't hurt; I understood what he meant. I understood what he had lost.

———

The next year, we started looking for an apartment to buy. We wanted to stay in Tribeca, far from our childhoods on the Upper East Side. In early 2001, James read about a building on the corner of Broadway and Chambers Street being converted to condominiums. It was an old state office building and sat across from the Tweed Courthouse, catty-corner from the Sun Building, and two blocks north of the Woolworth Building—the landmarks of our first date. It was also the original site of the Manhattan Project and still had Ellen's, a famous coffee shop, in its lobby, a meeting place for mayors and councilmen, a place my father had frequented. James tracked down the number of the company developing the building, called the owner, and said we wanted to see it. We toured a four-bedroom apartment on the twenty-fifth floor that faced west to the Hudson River. There were still long wooden pews in what would be the kitchen and living room, ghosts of the administrative hearings that had taken place there in the years before we arrived.

The apartment was much bigger than I thought we needed, and Chambers Street felt too gritty to me, unlike the more residential part of Tribeca, farther west, where my brother and Charmaine lived. But James loved everything about it—the history, the views, the proximity to subways, the authentic urban feel of the neighborhood. We decided to buy it. We would have to wait more than a year for the apartment to be ready for us—the norm in large building conversions.

My primary assets were held in two trusts that could be accessed, with the trustees' consent, for a legitimate purpose. I asked the trustees of the smaller trust, given to me by my mother's stepfather, for permission to use the trust's assets, in their entirety, to buy the apartment. They agreed. When we closed, I listed my name and James's name as joint owners, even though he had not contributed to the purchase. I was happy to be able to do it. It felt like an offering to him, to our marriage, to the family we were going to create. And I thought that was what you did when you were married— share everything.

———

I started trying to get pregnant the same year. I was serious about it, testing for ovulation, taking my temperature daily, creating charts. James was equally excited to have a baby. It took eight months, the wait increasing our excitement when I finally got a positive test on August 25, my father's birthday. My appointment to check for a heartbeat was scheduled for September 12, 2001.

I witnessed the terror attacks of September 11 from the south-facing picture window in my office on Beach Street, twenty blocks from the World Trade Center. After the second plane hit the South Tower, I called James at his office in Midtown. I was still on the phone with him when the towers fell. I screamed.

James left his office and started running south, in his shirtsleeves and nice shoes, against a tide of people walking north, away from the wreckage. He ran four miles to get to me, earning hot, bleeding blisters that stayed on his feet for weeks. When he arrived at my office, we held each other amid the sounds of sirens—police, fire, EMS—racing down Varick Street.

Within an hour, we knew we had to leave the area, to join the tide moving north. My brother drove us and Charmaine uptown, retracing James's steps back up Park Avenue, to Susan's apartment. When James and I looked at each other in the bright sunlight of the Upper East Side, we saw that we were covered in ash. It had settled on us during the short walk to my brother's garage.

My obstetrician kept my appointment the next day. James and I waited outside her office on East 67th Street, sitting together on the curb, watching a line of people form at a blood bank across the street. Only a day after the attack, New Yorkers still believed there were survivors, that there would be people they could help.

My doctor let us into the building, into her empty office, and did the ultrasound. We heard the steady thump of Finn's heartbeat. As we exited her office, we felt strange, our happy secret in my belly, shocked again by the reality of what had happened, our fear about what was to come. I felt James's protection in the face of the unknown, his care for me, and

I clung to it, I clung to him, the same way I would nineteen years later, during the first days of the pandemic.

We stayed at Susan's apartment for three weeks while Tribeca remained evacuated. When we returned to our rental on Worth Street in October, the air was thick with a terrible smell—organic, metallic, human. James bought air purifiers, believing they were enough to protect me and the baby, but I was too anxious. We moved back uptown for another month, returning for good in November.

I loved being pregnant and had a voracious appetite. Once we were back in our apartment, we went to Chinatown twice every weekend for barbecued pork buns, my most intense craving. I took the subway uptown for the Melon's bacon cheeseburgers of my youth, and to Häagen-Dazs for hot-fudge sundaes.

As my due date approached, I started to feel uncomfortable. I was gaining weight rapidly (a rate faster than I could blame on my eating), and I had a sharp pain under my right ribs. My obstetrician dismissed my complaints, and I progressed to almost forty weeks, with an increasing sense that something was wrong. When I went into labor, a resident diagnosed me with HELLP syndrome, a variant of pre-eclampsia that results in the death of the mother or baby in twenty-five percent of cases. The pain under my ribs was my liver, swollen with toxins. I was induced and the labor was frightening, my blood pressure skyrocketing with every contraction. My mother, Susan, and James were all there, all scared. For reasons I still don't understand, the obstetrician on duty (not my doctor) decided against a C-section.

Finn was born at 3:43 p.m on May 4, two days before my thirty-third birthday. I was shocked when they announced his sex; I was certain he would be a girl. As James held our new baby, he wiped away a tear and said, "I recognize him." They were identical, father and son: the same nose, eyes, chin. Finn was healthy, but I was not yet in the clear, experiencing HELLP episodes for several days, a phenomenon my obstetrician told us was impossible. She didn't come to see me until James demanded it on the third day. It was one of the only times I had ever heard him yell.

James was fully engaged with newborn Finn. He changed his diapers, sang to him with his guitar, and carried him proudly around our neighborhood in our BabyBjörn. We spent hours trying to get Finn to sleep, taking turns rocking him, pacing the length of our apartment. James started filming Finn with a small video camera and, with the help of a friend, created a movie for his first birthday—footage of him in the bath, crawling in the hallway of a hotel in Miami, on James's shoulders at the beach in Water Mill. James added a soundtrack specific to Finn—"Moon River" (the song he sang to my pregnant belly), Neil Young's "Heart of Gold," and Faith No More's "We Care a Lot."

Finn was seven months old when we moved into our new apartment on Broadway, just before Christmas in 2002. Susan helped us pay for a decorator who designed it in the minimalist style James and I liked, adding things from my family— my father's brass mirror above the fireplace, his treen objects placed among our combined books, photographs from both my father and grandfather in the hallways—Diane

Arbus and Paul Strand joining Sally Mann. We had a play-room, a laundry room with two stacked washers and dryers, a den. James had a proper office with a sitting area.

We were both eager for another baby. We started track-ing my ovulation cycle in careful charts for the second time, again waiting almost a year for a positive test. I had Evie in December 2004, a tiny, happy girl who sprouted white-blond hair and, eventually, huge front teeth. She was strong-willed as a toddler, certain of what she liked and didn't like, refus-ing most solid foods until we gave her bacon. We debated having a third child, unsure if we could handle it, but after Evie turned two, James called me from work and said, "Let's go for it. I'm a family man. I want another." I was thrilled; three kids felt like a commitment to a busy and happy life, different from my quiet childhood. Carrie was born in 2007. She was a sweet and easy baby. Unlike her brother and sister, she fell asleep immediately at night, her thumb in her mouth. She was in love with Evie from the moment she laid eyes on her. And Evie took her on, acting as a second mother, teach-ing her how to tie her shoes, how to wash her hands.

James was excited about each pregnancy. He gave me hep-arin shots, prescribed after a hematologist tied my HELLP syndrome to a blood-clotting disorder. He brainstormed girls' names with me. He brought me lattes and Krispy Kreme doughnuts on Sunday mornings and took Finn to play soccer in City Hall Park when I needed a nap. He was with me in the delivery rooms both times and sang "Moon River" to each girl as they were being cleaned up, before they were placed in my arms.

——

After Evie was born, James was promoted to president at the investment firm where he worked. As his professional obligations became more intense, he slowly, almost imperceptibly, moved away from doing things with the kids. He often came home late, exhausted, wanting only to eat dinner and go to bed. I could hear his footsteps from my perch in one of the kids' rooms where I was nursing a baby or trying to get a toddler to sleep. I could hear him opening the freezer, the ice clinking as he made himself a cocktail, always Svedka vodka on the rocks.

He didn't like the mundane tasks of taking care of kids and often said, with some humor, "I don't do bath, bed, or homework." And he didn't. Work came first, always. I knew other husbands like this, working seven days a week, but James seemed to be one extra degree of hardworking, one more turn on the dial of work obsessed. And I never forced him to engage or help. I let him skip curriculum nights, parent-visiting days, and most parent-teacher conferences. He went into the office every weekend, no matter what was going on with the kids.

We had made an unspoken bargain: he would work all the time and I would take care of the kids all the time. I resented this sometimes, usually when I was stressed, when one of the kids was sick, or when they were melting down over something. But most of the time, I liked his fervent commitment to his work. It was impressive, and it seemed honorable to me, to put so much time in, to be such a dutiful employee, to be working so hard for our family's long-term financial

security. It felt like he was taking care of us, each time he put
on his suit, each time he labored at his desk on a Saturday.

And I had help. I hired Tenzin as a babysitter when Finn
was two months old. She was a few years younger than I
was and had a daughter the same age as Finn. She didn't have
much experience in childcare, but I liked her immediately.
She was smart and warm and had a calm manner. Absolutely
nothing fazed her; she was the opposite of me as a mother.
I was very nervous, anxious about safety and schedules, always unsure if I was doing it right. When Finn was a baby,
Tenzin didn't have much to do; I took him to all his Music
Together classes, to his doctor's appointments and playdates.
I could barely take my eyes off him. But after the girls were
born, Tenzin and I were both busy, going in various direc-
tions for activities, splitting bedtime duties, alternating making dinner. It was the easy version, the privileged version,
of stay-at-home motherhood. Still, my days felt full, often
frantic, managing the kids and our life as a family.

Even as he receded from daily parenting, James was a kind
and sweet father, taking on the role of a visiting celebrity,
delighting the kids with his presence. He was always happy
to see them, breaking into a smile when they ran into a room,
embracing them, giving them nicknames—"Finshwin" for
Finn, "Babyface" for Evie, "Chichikakutani" for Carrie, I
can't remember why. He was never critical of them, never
angry. He took Finn to hockey practice at 5 a.m. on Saturday mornings for several years, and to Rangers games,
where they wore matching jerseys. He brought the girls to
musicals—they saw *Mamma Mia!* five times—and for soup
dumplings in Chinatown, rating each restaurant in a black-

and-white composition book. He started sourcing Hallow-
een candy in September, looking for hard-to-find brands
of sour candy to fill our bowl. He took each kid on trips
alone—Carrie to LA, Finn to Iceland, Evie to Rome. James
and Evie walked so many miles together on their trip, he
framed a map for her, a red line tracking the ground they
had covered. He continued to make movies of our life as a
family, using the footage we both collected, first on video
cameras and later on iPhones, including scores of his favorite music—Luna, Pavement, Dinosaur Jr. He made one for
every year, from 2003 to 2018.

The kids went to nursery school on Duane Street and then
to a coed Episcopal school on Fourth Avenue, a place with
uniforms and a traditional curriculum, similar to the schools
James and I had attended uptown. The kids each started in
junior kindergarten, tiny four-year-olds in navy pants and
jumpers, white shirts with school crests. They made friends,
as did I, and the school became a home for us. I volunteered
as a class parent, sold doughnuts at the fall festival, ran the
book fair.

I tried to keep some kind of professional life going, making sure I did the hours of continuing education to keep my
law license active, volunteering one day a week at a domestic violence nonprofit. I served on school boards, including the kids' school and the boarding school I had attended,
the latter a consuming role, requiring several days in New
Hampshire every quarter. I co-chaired the board of a local
education nonprofit. I developed an expertise in board gov-
ernance. Once Finn reached high school and the girls were
both in middle school, I started doing pro bono juvenile im-

migration cases with the mother of Evie's best friend, also a former big-firm lawyer.

But I never went back to paid work. James's job, combined with my anxiety about being available for my kids, made a return to the workforce feel impossible, like the road was blocked. I felt increasingly unskilled as a lawyer, and I had a glaring gap in my résumé. I sometimes felt like the worst kind of fraud; I was neither working nor a proper stay-at-home mother, since I had help with childcare and housework.

In 2012, a former colleague offered me a job at a large foundation he'd been hired to run. He believed in my competence, even while I didn't, and my skills seemed to be a fit. I was torn, but James was clear. He said, "You can't do that. You need to be here for the kids." The speed of his response, the lack of discussion, was startling. I had hoped he would encourage me to accept the job, that he would say, "Don't worry. We will figure it out. I will help." I felt a flash of resentment, but it shifted quickly. He was right. I needed to be home. We had to prioritize James's career. It was the way our family functioned. I turned down the job.

Most of the time, I was proud of my decision to stay home. I felt a rush of happiness every time I picked the kids up from school, seeing them in line to shake their teachers' hands, watching them grin as they spotted me waiting. I liked making them dinner, reading them books, baking Valentine's treats for their class. I hated parenting sometimes too—the frustrations, the meltdowns, the small failures. And I don't think I was always good at it. I lost my patience often. I hated the endless hours at the playground. I often worked on my laptop while my kids played on the floor next to my desk, reluctantly joining them when they begged me to sit down. But I felt like I was doing something important just by being there. I was giving them what I had longed for when I was a child.

———

After she divorced my father in 1972, my mother moved us to an apartment at 10 Gracie Square on the East River. It was a beautiful building, prewar and grand, but there was something foreboding about it. A car tunnel ran through its belly, from the entrance on East 84th Street to the exit on 83rd Street, and there was a deep, wide gulch between the building and the East River Esplanade, like a moat, filled with garbage no one would ever be able to reach. The building later became known for two suicides, one a young man, the other an older female writer. When I heard about the deaths, I thought about the darkness of that gulch, the private place to land.

Our apartment was in the middle of the building, in the second of three lobbies. It was called a "maisonette" because it occupied the first and second floors, with the front door off the lobby. It felt huge, with five bedrooms and a wide, curved staircase leading to the second floor. My mother loved rattan and bamboo furniture and there was a lot of it, along with sisal rugs and furniture upholstered in green, brown, and orange, her favorite colors. The dining room, almost as vast as the living room, was lined with kumquat trees. My mother's bedroom faced the river; my brother's and mine were on the other side, facing a maze of air condensers. There was a long hallway dividing us. My mother had a wide arrow painted in that hallway, stripes of primary colors, directing us from our side to hers.

As a young divorcée, my mother was scared and over-whelmed, trying to build a life alone with two toddlers. She enrolled at Sarah Lawrence and finished her BA, doing homework as we clamored around her, climbing onto her lap. After getting her college degree, she became an urban planner, first working for William Whyte, a pioneer in creating public spaces, and then on the team charged with developing Battery Park City. It was her deepest calling. She loved deciding how wide a brick in the esplanade should be, how narrow the arm of a bench, how to make spaces useful and enjoyable. In 1990, after getting her master's degree from Columbia, she was appointed to the City Planning Commission, and in 2002, Mayor Bloomberg made her the chair of the commission and head of the city's planning department, positions she held for twelve years. She was known for walking the streets of every neighborhood—she was familiar with every storefront, every streetlight—and for being tough with developers, demanding they add public spaces adjacent to their skyscrapers. She helped create the High Line elevated park and promenade and the Greenpoint-Williamsburg Waterfront, among other projects that transformed the city, but she is most proud of leading the most extensive rezoning of the five boroughs since 1961. Even now, she continues to work full-time, traveling the world, from Tampa to Turin, advising city governments on planning. My mother fought hard against the tide of expectation of who she would be, and she succeeded, creating a life that is true to her essential

nature. She has (almost) extinguished the moniker of "socialite," attached to her since her glamorous days in the Dakota,
an identity she hated.

My mother is very smart and hardworking. Her career
success is not surprising. But I think part of her intensity,
part of her ambition, was wanting to leave her mark on the
world after a childhood of feeling invisible. She grew up at
Kiluna Farm, the Paleys' estate in Manhasset, Long Island,
with her older brother, two half-siblings, and, sometimes,
her stepbrother and stepsister. The six children lived with
nannies in a house they called "the cottage," not with their
parents. My mother saw her own mother only once a month,
when she would appear in the cottage to put the kids to bed.
Her mother never hugged or kissed her. She never touched
her at all. Her distance was consistent with the era, with
that world; parents did not consider children central to their
lives. And the demands of my grandmother's marriage were
significant. But, still, the neglect, the coldness, is difficult to
explain, difficult to excuse.

Despite her childhood wound, my mother was warm, loving, and affectionate with me and my brother. She wanted to
do it right, to be interested in us, to hug us, to create memories with us. She put us to bed often, singing to us, checking
on me late at night when I developed childhood insomnia.
She made us crepes with apple jelly on Christmas morning and brought us toast with raspberry jam, cut into strips,
when we were sick. She filled our pantry with the junk cere-
als I loved and stocked the fridge with Sunkist, my brother's
favorite soda. She cared about our report cards and visited
us in boarding school. She could be short-tempered when

she was anxious, and she was always slightly guarded—her childhood made intimacy hard for her—but her mothering was a 180-degree shift from what she had been given herself.

When she was in her twenties and thirties, my mother was pursued by many men. She dated a succession of them until she met Stan, a tall, white-haired mogul who had founded a famous media company. Stan moved in with us in 1975, when I was six, appearing at breakfast in his bathrobe, my mother making him fried eggs. My brother and I loved him. He gave us a big and exciting life, introducing us to Pelé at the Meadowlands, taking us to the premiere of *Superman*, traveling by helicopter to his house in East Hampton and by private jet to his company's villa in Acapulco. But what we really loved was his presence, his way of being. He was all warmth and fun, and he wanted to be with us. He insisted we have family dinners. He waded into my brother's tantrums and my meltdowns with a fatherly gentleness. He spent hours with us on the floor, playing Battleship, Mastermind, the French card game Mille Bornes. He had two older kids who made short appearances, adding to the feeling that we had a complete family.

My mother and Stan married in 1979, after four years of living together, and divorced in 1981, separating the month we moved into a new apartment on Park Avenue (we spent only one night there). My mother left him, for reasons I now understand, including infidelity. But my brother and I felt the loss deeply. It proved too hard for Stan to keep seeing us, especially after he remarried, and he gradually faded from our lives. After he died of prostate cancer in 1992, his wife sent us two of his ties, mementos we suspected went to hundreds of people (he had a lot of ties). We weren't invited to his private funeral. It made sense; we hadn't seen him for several years and we were ex-stepchildren, a label without importance. But it hurt.

After her divorce from Stan, my mother had a series of boyfriends, each one joining us for a time, competing with us for her attention. I didn't like this, the appearance of new men in the apartment, on our vacations, at her rental houses in Connecticut. She met her long-term boyfriend, the one who would stay for thirty years, when I was in college.

As a shy and awkward kid, I didn't have many friends and I had trouble convincing the friends I did have to walk the many long blocks east to our apartment. In his preteen years, my brother disappeared into the world of Atari video games and then elected to go live with my father and Susan full-time until he went to boarding school. This left me on my own with our mother and our nanny.

At my mother's apartment, we always had a live-in nanny. The first was Cece, an older woman who was partially blind, and then Rose, a woman from Northern Ireland who moved in when I was in third grade. Rose spoke with an Irish lilt, wore very tight jeans, even tighter sweaters, and dyed her hair platinum blond, using a box of Clairol every month in our shared sink. She said she was thirty, but I suspected, based on the lines in her face, that she was much older. She was very strict and very mean.

Rose made me go to Saint Stephens, our local Catholic church, at least three times a week, insisting I put my allowance—two folded dollar bills—in the wicker basket they brought around during Mass, forcing me into the confession booth long before I had sins to confess. She brushed my hair after my required nightly showers, pulling far too hard, yelling if I had a single knot (I had many), ignoring my tears, sometimes hitting the side of my head with the hard part of the brush. She told me I was stupid when I didn't know that the stain in my underwear was my first period.

I was terribly embarrassed to have a nanny at all, especially one who was waiting for me outside my school, side by side with the stay-at-home mothers. When I was in second grade, in a scheme to stop my nanny from picking me up, I told my mother that all my classmates were taking the public bus alone, and she agreed to let me do it. At eight years old, I boarded the 86th Street crosstown bus, early in the morning and after school, knowing where to get off only because of certain landmarks, like the orange curtains in the window of the Madison Avenue deli.

For years, I didn't say anything to anyone about Rose's meanness, or about my embarrassment in having a nanny. I endured it silently, knowing that Rose would make things harder for me if I complained. Finally, when I turned fourteen, I told my mother everything, confessing my torment all at once as she stood in her bathroom applying mascara. I described the punishing hours at church, the hairbrush, the small comments Rose made to me about my appearance, about my lack of friends.

My mother had no idea. She fired Rose that day.

After that, my mother stopped going out. She cooked dinner for me every night, using long-dormant skills she'd acquired as a young woman studying at Le Cordon Bleu in Paris. She made perfectly grilled lamb chops and buttery mashed potatoes, veal scallopini with rice in a champagne cream sauce, always comforting food that she prepared quickly and easily. I'd set the table, pour her a glass of wine, and we'd watch *Family Feud* as we ate, competing to hit the buzzer first, slapping our hands on the table.

Growing up, I had three parents who loved me. They called me every night when we were apart. There was fun, there was happiness. But there was also a lot of quiet. My mother's apartment always felt dark, shut down, like it was abandoned or waiting for a real family to arrive. I remember many solitary afternoons and evenings, doing my homework at my little desk with a rolltop cover, reading *Deenie* and *Harriet the Spy* on my bedroom floor, spending hours watching sitcoms, *The Love Boat,* and MTV, alone on my mother's bed. I had a running commentary with myself, creating stories, imaginary friends, trying to keep myself company.

I yearned, deeply, for a normal family, a stay-at-home mother, a lively household with many kids, a life with no divorces, no mean nannies, no split time, no loneliness. So, I became what I'd always wanted for myself: a mother who stood in the schoolyard, day after day, waiting for her kids, with chocolate chip cookies in her hand.

————

Susan, my brother, and I sold our house in Water Mill in 2005. After my father's death, we'd tried to share the house, but it brought out a host of tensions between us, primarily over the high cost of maintaining it. When a Wall Street titan made an incredible offer, we agreed it was time to sell. It was hard to let go of the house; it felt like letting go of my father. But it was also liberating to leave it behind. James and I didn't feel at ease in the Hamptons, at least not the modern version of it, which involved a lot of competing, dressing up, and traffic.

There was an expectation that we would have a country house, a place to go in the summer, a replacement for Water Mill. Most of our peers in New York, nearing forty, were buying summer homes. It wasn't just expectation; we wanted it—a respite from the city, a place to define ourselves, an investment in our life as a family. But we weren't sure where to go.

One night in our new apartment, my friend Lynn and her husband came over for dinner. Lynn and I had been close since boarding school, part of a tight group of six friends that also included Anna.

Lynn asked, "How about the Cape? Or the Vineyard?" She and her husband had just bought a house on Cape Cod. They spoke about the magic of New England summers, the clamming and the crabbing, the beaches and the sunsets.

James and I looked at each other. Somehow, we hadn't thought of the Vineyard, even though we both had history on the island. James had spent his childhood summers at his grandparents' house in Edgartown. They'd sold it in the late 1980s, putting the proceeds into a small apartment in Manhattan, a trade that haunted James because he associated it with his family's financial decline. I'd spent the summer after my freshman year in college living in a ramshackle house in Vineyard Haven with six other girls, all of us working for a landscaping company. We spent our days weeding and mulching the yards of expensive houses and the late afternoons drinking peach wine coolers with the guys who mowed the lawns. We hitchhiked between towns and beaches, covering ourselves in the clay from the cliffs of Aquinnah, then named Gay Head. People called us "the seven island sisters." I loved it.

That night, after Lynn and her husband left, James and I looked for houses online. We found one that was listed by four different agents, on a lake five minutes outside of Vineyard Haven, a location that appealed to James—he could have a mooring for a boat, and the lake had a cut to the open water of Vineyard Sound. He loved boating. He kept a small Boston Whaler in Battery Park, taking it out every weekend to explore different canals and waterways around Manhattan and Brooklyn.

James flew up to see the house during a snowstorm in February. I couldn't go because Evie was only six weeks old. The broker picked James up at the airport and drove him down a long, snow-covered dirt road to the house.

He called me an hour later, as I sat nursing Evie. He said, "The house is a little weird, but the rest of it is magic."

We learned the house had been on the market for five years (thus the multiple listings), and the price, though still significant, had just been reduced. A local contractor had built the house on spec, designing it to mirror the double-doored, vaulted-ceilinged living room of Chip Chop, an estate owned by Mike Nichols and Diane Sawyer directly across the lake. The contractor built it as his dream house, and it had a distinctly wintry feel, with black countertops and an enormous brick pizza oven in the kitchen, and big splintery beams cutting the height of the ceiling in the living room, like a large ski chalet. And it was all upside down: the kitchen, living room, and primary bedroom were upstairs; the other bedrooms were downstairs.

As James walked across the lawn and out onto the dock, talking to me on his cell phone, he sounded elated. He spoke about raising our kids there, spending summers on the lake, adopting the island as our own. And doing our own thing, different from the Hamptons, different from my childhood. I was swept up with him, with his joy and certainty. We decided to make an offer, even though I had not seen the property. Within a few hours, our offer was accepted. I wired the money for the down payment.

My family thought I had lost my mind, leaving them, leaving the Hamptons, for an island they kept confusing with Nantucket, for a house I had never seen. I liked surprising them, making it clear that my priorities were James and our young family, making it clear I trusted James's opinion, his gut instinct about what was right for us.

My last trust, from my father's father, one that would have gone to my father if he were alive, matched the purchase price exactly, minus a small mortgage. The trustees agreed to release the funds. When we closed, I did exactly what I had done with the apartment: I listed James and myself as joint owners. I was happy to contribute something so meaningful to our family, to cure, in some way, James's heartache over having once lost a house on the very same island. And after five years of marriage, I believed even more strongly in our partnership, in our commitment to each other.

I finally saw the house in April. I carried baby Evie in my arms as James showed us each room, going up and down the stairs, his excitement palpable, nearly euphoric. As we stood in the living room, looking out at the lake, I put Evie on the floor in her car seat. Only a few minutes later, I looked down and saw that her pale skin was covered, head to toe, with hundreds of mosquitos. They were the result of an untended pond on the property, a mosquito breeding ground. I thought, *Oh my God, what have we done?*

We hired a contractor to remove the pizza oven, the black countertops, the beams. We added bead boarding, painted the walls and ceilings white, and stained the floors dark. We combined "his" and "hers" bathrooms into one large one. We filled in the mosquito-infested pond and thinned trees to see more of the lake. We enlisted the interior designer who worked on our apartment to decorate the house in blue and white, with some red, all comfortable and welcoming of small kids and wet bathing suits.

On the Vineyard, it is common to give a house a name, something related to the area, the road, a nearby body of water. James suggested we use the Indigenous name for our land, "Meadowpath," a word he discovered in the closing process. He designed a Meadowpath sign—navy and white, a wide *V* in the right corner to symbolize an osprey—and used an electric drill to secure it to our gate. The name became our most prized word. We used it for email addresses, streaming passwords, stationery. It symbolized everything we had built together—home, family, security, love.

———

We moved into the house with Finn, then four, and Evie, then eighteen months, in June of 2006. A colleague of James's

told him about a private tennis club, located only five minutes away from our new house. It was a generational place—
populated by families who had been coming for decades,
from Boston, Washington, DC, New York. It looked like
the Adirondacks with lots of trees and simple wood buildings with dark green trim. There was an inn, a playground, a
clubhouse, three piers, a small shop with penny candy. Members wore all white on the tennis courts and gathered for
cocktail parties in linen blazers and colorful dresses. I resisted
it at first; it felt intimidating in its clubbiness, its insularity.
My family had never joined country clubs on principle, and
I didn't play tennis. But James was wild about it—the tennis
culture, the people, the feel of the place, the life it would
provide for our family. Since I wasn't working and the kids
were little, we decided that I would stay on the island for the
summer and James would commute on weekends. The kids
needed a camp and friends, so I agreed that we should apply
for membership at the club. We became guest members, on
trial for three years until we could apply for full membership.

I dropped Finn off at the club's camp every morning in
his green Celtics jersey and shorts, the only outfit he would
wear that summer. I felt shy, not sure how to meet other parents, how to create friendships for the kids and myself. There
was something about the club—even the playground—that
felt impenetrable; everyone seemed to know one another, to
have plans, to engage in traditions we knew nothing about.
That first summer, James and I had no social life, neither invited anywhere nor extending invitations. We stayed home,
eating dinner with the kids, inviting family and friends from

New York to visit us every weekend, running what felt, at times, like a hotel.

Eventually, slowly, we got to know the parents of our kids' friends, then their friends, and we started to be accepted. We became permanent members. And then we embraced all of it. Finn and Evie rode their bikes a mile up the dirt road to meet up with gangs of kids their age. I held Carrie on my hip as I dropped them off at camp and tennis clinics. We jumped off the pier into Vineyard Sound in the late afternoons. The kids did the bunny hop and the limbo at club dances. We went to bonfires and sang folk songs. We combed one of the club's small beaches for sea glass and multicolored marbles, the latter an offering from a family who launched hundreds of them from their deck into the water. I hosted an art class, hiring a local teacher, and invited kids of all ages to paint large canvases on our lawn. Our sixteen-year-old babysitter went to pick up a dozen pizzas while I poured white wine for the mothers, who were now my friends.

James and I socialized throughout the summer, attending cocktail and dinner parties every weekend. The couples were kind and a lot of fun. We kept an eye out for one another's kids, bandaging scraped knees, giving gentle scoldings when we saw them biking without helmets. Later, when the kids became teenagers, we helped one another track them down at midnight and shared harrowing stories of their first encounters with alcohol. The women were universally well-educated, but most, like me, had left the workforce. This felt good; in New York, I felt conflicted, and embarrassed, about having paused my legal career. I didn't feel this way on the Vineyard, surrounded by smart women who had made the same choice. There was a sense of being exactly where we should be, giving our kids a magical experience, where they could roam freely, safe and protected, summer after summer. At the time, I didn't pay attention to the fact that almost everyone at the club was married. Out of more than a hundred people, I knew of only three who were single or divorced.

James flew up to the island every weekend and stayed for a week in early August. Many of the other husbands at the club kept the same schedule. On Friday evenings, he appeared as the sun softened, walking toward the house carrying his briefcase, his jacket on his arm, his shirtsleeves rolled up, grinning. The kids and I ran down our brick path to hug him, our dog jumping up on our huddle. He grilled hamburgers for the kids while I made pasta, their favorite meal and our Friday-night ritual, the burgers always without buns at the kids' request, the juices mixing into the pasta. James made himself his cocktail of vodka on the rocks, poured me a glass of wine, and we sat on our porch watching the sun set, on the left side of the lake's cut in June, on the right by early September. The kids ran around the lawn with Popsicles and soccer balls until it was dark.

James discovered that the shallow area of the lake was rich with clams. We bought a shellfish license from town hall and spent many weekend afternoons feeling out the hard shells with our toes, the kids diving below the surface to collect each one. James made linguine alle vongole, spending hours on the broth, chopping the clams and piles of parsley, saving the smallest, prettiest clams to adorn the top of the bowl. He found grape leaves on our property and stuffed them with a mixture of ground beef and herbs, folding them with an obsessive meticulousness, and grilling them on our deck. He took us on boating adventures every weekend on his new Chris-Craft: tubing in Lambert's Cove, up to Menemsha for lobster rolls from Larsen's and fried shrimp from the Bite, over to Silver Beach on Naushon Island to see my boarding-school roommate, a member of the family that owned the island. James played a lot of tennis, often twice a day, becoming friends with other husbands who were equally passionate about the sport.

In 2008, Susan bought us an eight-acre plot of land adjacent to our house. We wanted to secure our privacy and have space for the kids to build houses as adults. The new plot was all forest—oak trees, pine trees, brush. James was entranced with it. He created winding paths, pruned trees with a long pole saw, and sprayed every weekend for poison ivy, wearing a Roundup backpack with a nozzle. He said it would take him many years to make the paths perfect for the girls' weddings. He imagined walking them through the woods to a small beach on the lake, steps from the osprey pole. He named the beach for Finn, and carved Evie's initials in a fallen tree trunk beside the boardwalk. He found boulders in the woods and named them for each kid, the biggest for Carrie. He taught them how to find their rocks using his carefully tended paths.

He kept investing in our Vineyard imprint, year after year. In 2018, he designed a large addition to the garage to house his extensive collection of motorcycles and forestry equipment. He included a garden on top of the addition for me, raised beds we filled with herbs and tomatoes and flowers. In 2019, he planted blueberry and raspberry bushes on the edge of the property, plants that take several years to bear fruit.

———

As we raised the kids in New York, James and I were firmly in the present tense, with days, weeks, years going by, both slowly and quickly. We played Whack-a-Mole with kid issues—a failed Spanish test, lice, science projects, stomach flus. I was covered in breast milk, then baby food, then spaghetti sauce; cribs gave way to toddler beds and then real beds; strollers were replaced by scooters, which were then given away. We planned our family vacations, first to easy destinations like Florida and then as far away as Hawaii. We decided which dinner invitations we would accept, which we would decline. We went out most Friday nights, just the two of us, always in our neighborhood. I loved these dinners. We always talked easily. It always felt fun.

We had normal stresses and two great heartbreaks. In 2011, Lynn, my best friend from boarding school, was diagnosed with a rare and terminal cancer when she was pregnant with her fourth child. She had a mastectomy, delivered her baby, and started chemotherapy to try to extend the time she had left—a maximum of two years. Another member of our group from boarding school had died thirteen years earlier from brain cancer. She and Lynn were very similar—athletic, outgoing, famously funny; it seemed unfathomable that we could lose them both. I vowed to be present for Lynn in a way I hadn't been for our other friend, too immature in my twenties to really support her. Treatment tore Lynn down in all the big ways but also in very small ones—I can still hear her voice, having to say her name and birth date over and over again to doctors, nurses, and technicians at the hospital, waiting hours for a chemo bag or a scan, then driving in maddening traffic back to her house in the suburbs, trying to reserve some energy to be present for her kids, all younger than eight years old. She would call me often in the middle of the night, wanting to talk about her impending death, about the unbearable prospect of leaving her children. If I made any attempt to be positive, saying there would be a miracle, that she would live, she would say, "Flo, stop, I am going to die."

I said goodbye to her on July 30, 2013, at her house on Cape Cod. I knew her death was imminent, but I was still undone by it, by the tidal wave of grief I felt when I was told the next day that she was gone, by the overwhelming sadness that remained for years afterward. James was loving and supportive, patient with my feelings, understanding what it felt like to lose such a close friend. He had carried the grief of Mark's death for fourteen years at that point; it had become a part of him, dimming him in many ways—his joy, his hope for adventure, his pleasure in the unpredictable.

James's father died in 2016 from an undiagnosed illness, most likely cancer (he had refused to go to a doctor). James sat at his bedside for two weeks, arranging round-the-clock nursing care, changing his father's clothing and sheets himself, holding his father's hand. James was heartbroken by the loss, crying in my arms. It was only the third time I'd ever seen him cry—the first when Mark died, the second when

Finn was born. I felt like he was grieving both his father's death and what had happened to his father in life—his break- down, his financial failure, his retreat from the world.

During the ups and downs of our life together—as a cou- ple, as parents—I felt like James and I were entirely united, a team riding the waves together, a deep current of love and commitment binding us, accompanying each other through life. When I felt mad at him, or frustrated with him, it never lasted for long. Within a couple of hours, I felt the sensa- tion of love washing away any anger, any annoyance. It was a feeling I'd never had with anyone else.

———

As James moved deeper into the investment world, I handed more of our financial life over to him. He understood the stock market, balance sheets, taxes. He could have the con- versations with bankers and lawyers that I hated. Bankers and lawyers had always been tied up, in my mind, with the tur- moil of my father's death. He told me how much money to wire into our checking account every month, the amount to pay in taxes. He dealt with the gas company, the landscaper, the accountants, the bookkeeper—anything and everything to do with money.

James was protective of me financially, always speaking up for my interests with my family. He also kept a sharp eye on our spending. Our transfers into our checking account, always equal, were small numbers; we were often in over- draft after I paid our regular bills, requiring another transfer. James preferred this scenario because he thought it made us more aware of our spending, what he called our "burn rate."

He became agitated if our joint Visa bill was too high, a vacation too expensive. At hotels, he made me smuggle food to him from the breakfast buffet—hard-boiled eggs in paper coffee cups, a muffin in my pocket—so that we didn't have to pay one more cover. He asked me to annotate our joint credit card bills, explaining each charge in tiny print. Because of his anxiety, his watchfulness, I hid some things—the kids' clothes, their birthday and Christmas presents, my clothes—paying for them on my own credit card, the Amex I paid myself, the one we didn't split, the one I didn't have to show him. My family paid other expenses for us, including school tuition and college savings plans for each child. It felt like another offering to James, taking these weighty costs off his shoulders.

He had excessive moments too, usually when it related to his passions. With his salary, he could finally afford to buy the things he loved and he didn't hold back: a dozen rare Rolex watches, several motorcycles, rare coins, custom suits from Zegna, a small vintage boat that had been used in *Live and Let Die,* and expensive red wine, hundreds of bottles that we added to the ones I had inherited from my father, storing all of them in a climate-controlled facility in New Jersey. We acquired other things together—Berenice Abbott photographs of downtown I gave James on his birthday, pets (a gecko, multiple fish, a Goldendoodle), piles of our children's artwork, books, Amex points—the stuff you accumulate when you are married, have kids, and have money. Our apartment, though still modern and minimalist, was filled with all of it. Layer upon layer of life, of comfort and security.

I paid our bills online and signed our tax returns, but

slowly, I lost touch with both the big picture and the details of our financial life, depending on James to tell me what to do. I felt some shame about it, about not being involved, about not asking questions. But I was afraid I wouldn't understand it, that it was too complicated for me, even though I was a former corporate lawyer. I settled into the vagueness, the luxury and privilege of not knowing.

And part of me liked it, the handing over. James's care for our money felt like his contribution to our family, the way he showed his love and commitment to me and the kids. There was something romantic about it too—the smart and honorable man, the devoted husband and father, shouldering this part of our life. I had my own bucket of responsibility—the kids, their school, the meals, the homework, the bedtimes—so it made sense that he would take on our finances. We were dividing and conquering.

———

In 2015, when the kids were thirteen, eleven, and eight, James led the sale of the company where he was president, the one founded by my uncle, to another fund. James said the deal was a success, but not a big one. He had several offers for a new job but decided to go work for a hedge fund founded by a childhood friend, a famously successful enterprise housed in a handsome building in the Nolita neighborhood of downtown Manhattan.

James joined the firm in the spring of 2016. He did well there, rising quickly through the upper ranks, becoming the fund's chief client officer and chair of the executive committee by 2018. He told me the fund elected partners every two years, in even numbered years. Partnership at a New York City hedge fund is a life-changing accomplishment; if the fund is successful, the partner's take-home pay can be many millions of dollars a year. Given the firm's geographic proximity to our kids' school, several partners at the fund sent their children there. Their names always appeared at the top of the page of donors in the school's annual report—a very small, elite group. They owned some of the most beautiful town houses in New York. Partnership was something James and I talked about often, the goal of his career, the finish line, the reward, the reason for his absence from so many family responsibilities.

Two years after James started at the fund, in December 2018, I sat in a pew at the church attached to our children's school, waiting for Evie's eighth-grade Christmas pageant to begin. James called me on my cell phone.

"I didn't make partner," he said, his voice a low whisper. "They said I haven't been here long enough. They said I would make it next time." He sounded crestfallen. I sat between other parents and grandparents, the phone pressed to my ear, frozen.

I spoke as softly as I could, "When will that be?"

He answered, "Two years. December 2020."

I was devastated for him, knowing how disappointed he was, knowing how long two years would feel.

———

Seven months after the pageant, in July 2019, we met with our lawyer at her office in Hudson Yards. She had shared an agenda for the meeting with us, a list of routine estate planning matters. The last entry on the list was "Extinguish Prenuptial Agreement." Over the years, we had discussed getting rid of the prenup, agreeing that it was no longer fair to me, given James's career success, given the fact that I had emptied my trusts to purchase our homes.

The morning of the meeting, as James brushed his teeth in our bathroom, he turned to me.

He said, "Let's table the prenup for now. We have too many other things to do. Let's focus on the wills. I want to leave everything to you. Not in trust for the kids."

I was touched that he wanted to leave me his assets outright, a change from our prior plan. It didn't seem like a problem to delay getting rid of the prenup, to wait for a better time.

I said, "Okay."

At the meeting, our lawyer told us that Susan could no longer pay the kids' school tuition; her assets were too depleted. We nodded, not surprised. We'd had a long run, lucky to have this expense covered for us, along with their college savings plans. It was time for us to take it on.

After we discussed our wills, James stood up to leave. He said, "I have to get back to my office."

Our lawyer never had a chance to say, "We can't find the prenup."

———

As James entered his fifties, he seemed to be in the prime of his life. He knew who he was and how he wanted to move through the world. He had become increasingly eccentric as the years went by, almost like he had shifted onto the spectrum, or into the mindset of a sixty- or seventy-year-old man, but he showed no embarrassment about it. He went to bed at 9 p.m. and tracked his sleep cycles obsessively on his Oura Ring, reporting the results to me every morning. He didn't like small talk, and he was always the first to leave a dinner or cocktail party, entirely confident in his right to do so. He was more and more obsessed with forestry, with the ospreys, and with tennis. He played at a court in Grand Central on Tuesdays and Sundays and watched tennis on the Tennis Channel almost every night as he ate pretzels dipped in mustard. I felt protective of this side of him, wanting to shield and smooth over his awkwardness in social situations, with the kids, with my family. I thought this was my lot—a husband who was older than his years, maybe not so much fun, but someone I loved deeply. We would grow old together, welcoming grandchildren, spending more and more time on the Vineyard. He would follow the ospreys, clean the paths, trim the trees, sit with me as the sun set, content in the life we had built together.

He was even-tempered and steady throughout our marriage, rarely raising his voice. I never had to worry about moods or outbursts, as I had in my childhood. I felt intimate with him, emotionally and physically, from the first day to the last. Still, I was conscious that there was a piece of him that I couldn't quite reach, a chunk of mystery. I liked this, the unknown piece, the feeling that there was something I had not yet discovered about my partner of two decades. It was sexy. It kept me interested.

The image of the eccentric old man, the unreachable man, is not the complete picture, though. There was another side of James, one that emerged when he started working for the hedge fund in Nolita. He was friends with a group of wealthy men who were fellow tennis fanatics, men we both liked. He played with them at the Grand Central court and had drinks with them afterward at Cipriani, a restaurant overlooking the concourse and the clock, the site of our engagement, often missing our family dinners for another round. They went on trips together, tennis and hunting weekends, transported to every location on a private plane. James seemed more confident when he was with these men, even cocky. There was a sheen of entitlement when he returned home.

Our physical relationship, once so hot, cooled considerably over twenty years, but not in a way that felt cold. It always felt romantic between us, and tender. He was not always affectionate, but I felt his love like a vibration around us. Sometimes, even in the months right before he left, he would look at me across a table, stand slightly, and put his hand gently on my cheek, his mouth slightly open, the way he had looked at me, and touched me, the night of our first kiss. Even after two decades of marriage, I loved how he smelled, how soft his skin was, the way he walked. Whenever I saw him from afar, approaching on the street, or stepping into the school gym just in time for a play or concert, my heart leapt. He would sit down next to me on the bleachers and our hands would immediately intertwine, his cold from outside, mine warm. I'd put my head on his shoulder.

When we heard about infidelities and divorces, he assured me it would never happen to us. He said that we were different from other couples because we were so compatible, so similar—quiet, cerebral, happiest at home. He told me, every day, that he loved me. He asked me often, "I make you so happy, right?"

He never told me, not once, that he was discontent in our marriage, unhappy with me, or struggling in our life together.

I wonder now, *Did I make up the love story, the tale of our commitment to each other, carrying it around under my arm like a prized book?* I'd believed in that narrative, referring to it daily in my mind, telling others the story of how we met, how long we'd been married, confident that I was someone who had experienced true love, who had a marriage that was strong and happy. There was nothing tangible to refute it, no sign that the cord between us was broken, or even fraying, no indication that he was unhappy.

But what if the story I told myself wasn't true? What if he always had a different story?

Part III

Osprey couples mate within days of meeting, producing two to four eggs. The female "broods" the eggs, warming them, caring for them. The male continues to gather material for the nest, delivering it back to the female. He hunts to sustain them, always fresh fish—trout, bluefish, menhaden.

Osprey eggs incubate for four to five weeks and hatch in the late spring. The chicks grow rapidly, reaching their full size and weight within forty days. They leave the nest ("fledge") in midsummer. Before flying for the first time, they practice, flapping their wings while holding on to the nest with their talons. Eventually, they let go, first hovering over the nest like a helicopter, then taking short, cautious flights. Soon they learn to fish for themselves. At this stage, the offspring are called "juveniles." They are distinguishable from their parents because their eyes are orange (rather than yellow) and their wing feathers have white, scalloped edges.

The juveniles hone their skills for the remainder of the summer, fishing with more accuracy, venturing farther from the nest, until the cooler air and shorter days of September signal that it is time to leave the island.

———

After James left on the seaplane, after the girls and I ate our takeout dinner, I sat at our card table in the corner of the living room, drinking lemon ginger tea and doing a *New Yorker* jigsaw puzzle of Central Park. Puzzles were one of the only ways I could pass time—reading, or even television, felt too hard.

The card table, now cleared of James's papers and laptop, was filled with hundreds of puzzle pieces. I had completed the edges and was working on the trees in the middle of the picture, a mix of green, red, and brown leaves. I tried to focus on one piece at a time, joining two and then three, starting on another pair, another set, plodding through it. The image on the box—a lake in the center of the park, a couple in a rowboat—made me long for New York, for home.

Carrie came into the living room, her step always surprisingly heavy for such a small girl, and said, "I don't know about this other lady." She said a name I didn't recognize, something that sounded like fruit.

I looked up from the table, "Who?"

She said, "The one Daddy cheated on you with." I gripped the puzzle piece I was holding.

Carrie said that before James had left, sometime after Evie's slingshot lesson and before his basement searching, while I was making the turkey sandwich, she had asked him, "Did you cheat on Mommy?"

He said, "Yes."

She asked, "What is her name?"

He gave Carrie the name she had just given me. It was not the alliterative one I knew, the name that had tormented me since he left, the one I googled multiple times a day, staring at her face on the screen, trying to understand why he had chosen her over me. In addition to having a profile on LinkedIn, she had posted three photos on Facebook—a vacation photo on a boat (her dark hair pushed back with sunglasses), a photograph of a tropical drink (served in a coconut and decorated with an orchid), and her profile photo (another vacation shot, this one at a zoo). She was fifteen years younger than me, but not a younger version of me. We looked like the opposite of each other, in height, coloring, style. I thought, *He wants something different.*

I also found her husband's photograph and work history online. He was as accomplished as she was, with an impressive title at a well-known technology company. He had close-cropped hair, pale skin, and looked young too—so young, they could have been our children. I learned, by paying a fee on an address-search site, that they lived in a neighborhood adjacent to ours, in a high-rise I would be able to see from the window of my bedroom when I returned to New York.

I had not reached out to the woman or her husband since the night of the voicemail and the ambulance. Her husband didn't text or call me again either. An older friend, a lawyer, advised me against any contact. He said, "It will become messy very quickly, and it will only lead to more misery. It could also, possibly, make you look bad in front of a judge when you divorce." His advice felt like a clear, defined path, one that felt dignified. I vowed that I would never contact the husband again; I would never have words with the woman who was sleeping with my husband. But still they haunted me, these phantom figures, the supporting actors in the story of my marriage ending.

I picked up my phone from the table and texted James.

"What is this name you gave Carrie? Are there two women?"

He replied immediately, "No. She has two names." He spelled out the name she had been given at birth, and the alliterative one she used at work. His tone, even in text, felt scolding, like I should have known this basic fact. His loyalty was with her now, not us.

When James made his speech to the girls in the living room, to Finn on the phone, he didn't mention the affair. We discussed it beforehand, the decision to leave it out. He didn't want to tell them, and I agreed. It felt sordid, talking about their father sleeping with someone else, and I thought, *If we hide it, they will be more likely to forgive him.* I was protecting him. But he had told Carrie. He had changed course without telling me.

I was too stunned to feel angry. And too worried about Carrie trying to absorb this new name in our family story. Carrie looked almost exactly like me as a kid, but we were different. She had the courage to ask her father those questions, demanding the truth. I would never have asked.

I stood up from the table and said, "I'm so sorry. I should have told you earlier." She was sitting upside down in an upholstered chair near the fireplace, her head hanging off the seat, her small bare feet bouncing in the air. I said, "Let's go talk to Evie."

She said, "She already knows. She said she knew for a long time."

I learned later that Evie had known since she'd read a text on my iPad, in the first days after James left, before I learned to turn off notifications. She had carried that knowledge, that load, while I was pretending everything was fine, while she did her schoolwork and played her cello, while she cooked for me and her sister, trying to keep us afloat. She had tried to tell me in her own way, sending that late-night text. But I had not understood.

———

I struggled to get out of bed each morning. It was like a weighted blanket was on me, preventing me from moving, from standing up. I kept the television on, letting it run for hours, from early local news to *Good Morning America* to daytime talk shows. The girls made their own breakfasts, usually cereal that they brought to their computers, eating it during their first remote class, leaving the milk on the kitchen counter to grow warm. By late morning, I knew they would start looking for me. I had to get up, open the shades, make my bed, change out of my pajamas, unload the dishwasher, put the milk back in the fridge. It all felt hard, like I was moving through mud.

At some point in late April, at my friend Anna's urging, I made myself get up before the talk shows started, promising her I would try a short walk through the woods, down our dirt road to a small public beach. I still felt heavy and slow, but the cold air felt good, moving my legs felt good.

I went a little farther the next day, out to the asphalt road, to our mailbox. Then a mile to the pharmacy in town. Then two miles, down Franklin Street, up Main Street. I logged my steps on my phone, the numbers increasing, bars turning from red to green.

Within a couple of weeks, I was doing a wide loop around Vineyard Haven and West Chop, totaling nearly eight miles every day, religiously, in sunshine, rain, and, once, hail. I alternated the direction of the loop, one day clockwise, heading to the water, the next counterclockwise, toward town. My new Blundstone boots started to wear in, showing the miles, the ground I was covering, dusted white from saltwater. I always included a stretch of beach in the walk, looking for sea glass in the width of wet sand.

Susan and I had collected sea glass together since I was a little girl. I had a tall jar filled with it, on a table to the left of the front door, with a silver plaque Susan had inscribed with every person who had contributed to the collection—me, Susan, her mother, my father, my brother, James, Finn, Evie, Carrie. On my walks, I had a high bar for what I would keep—the glass had to be completely smooth, no slick or sharp edges, and bigger than a quarter. I found a piece almost every time, the common dark green and brown glass, and the rarer colors—aqua, sky blue, pale pink. I dropped each piece in the jar when I returned home, a bounty, a purpose to my journey.

Most of the time, I didn't see anyone else on my walks. If I did see someone, usually going the other direction, one of us would cross the street or dirt road to create distance between us, lifting our masks to cover our mouths as we passed. I always walked up or down William Street. It was the prettiest street in town, with big white clapboard houses, picket fences, porches, and wide lawns. A small Episcopal church stood at the top of the street. In the summer, it was the site of the Friday lobster roll sale, a wildly popular event. The church was quiet during the pandemic, its doors locked, but I stopped in front of it whenever I passed, looking up at the cross on the pitched roof.

I was an obedient Catholic for many years after Rose left my mother's house. Lynn and I went to Mass every Sunday at the Catholic church in our boarding-school town. We took Communion, put money in the collection basket, kneeled in the confession booth. I prayed every night, reciting the Lord's Prayer, and believed in a kind but censorious God. This religiousness was strange—my Catholic father didn't go to church as an adult; my mother, an Episcopalian who converted to Catholicism in the wake of her second divorce, never imposed it on me. My strict devotion had come from Rose, her admonitions still in my head.

My first year in college, I took a class about the New Testament and discovered that so much of what Jesus taught in the Bible—compassion, inclusion, and spirituality—conflicted with the punishing, rote rules of my childhood in the Catholic Church, my life with Rose. I shed my religious devotion abruptly and completely. In my adult life, I have only attended church for baptisms, weddings, and funerals.

Standing on William Street, looking up at the cross atop the Episcopal church, I didn't pray, but I thought about the people I worried about—my mother alone at her house in Bellport on Long Island, Finn in Sag Harbor, the girls, sometimes even James. I thought about the friends checking on me every day. My thought loop, moving through these tender connections, became its own kind of prayer. As I walked away, the Catholic girl in me emerged for a moment: I made the sign of the cross, my fingers on my forehead, my heart, each shoulder.

I started to depend on the walks, like they were fuel. I'd read that the best way to handle a heartbreak of any kind was to move through it, rather than around it. This made sense to me. I think I moved around my father's death, unable to understand or face it completely. But in my long, solitary loops, I felt like I was literally walking through my sadness, the muck of it, day after day. I got to know it. I screamed in the woods. I cried openly on the deserted sidewalks of Vineyard Haven. I lay down on the cold sand of the beach, midwalk, in anguish. The pandemic allowed this, in the cancellation of regular life, in the absence of noise, in the quiet.

———

I went to the local grocery store every Thursday. I put Evie's list and mine in the pocket of my jeans, her list always longer, her sweet teenage print filling the page. Before I left, I cleaned the kitchen thoroughly—throwing out old food, wiping the refrigerator shelves, scrubbing the range. I had replaced my natural cleaning products with Clorox, Lysol, S.O.S., Dawn, still believing that the virus lived on objects, that I could kill it with chemicals. I hated cleaning, but I liked the order and ritual of the task, doing it on the same day at the same time, starting fresh when I returned with my grocery bags, placing eggs and vegetables and yogurt onto clean shelves—each step giving me a sense of control.

My trips to the grocery store felt like weekly ventures into battle. The island was still sparsely populated, there were no lines outside the door, but the atmosphere inside the store was tense. The aisles were marked with one-way arrows, and there were lists of rules about where to stand at checkout, when to unload our carts. We gave one another space, politely waiting to select our bunch of bananas until the person ahead of us had moved on. But it did not feel like camaraderie. There was an air of suspicion, of needing to protect ourselves against one another.

At checkout, before starting to scan my items, the clerk always asked, "Do you have an island number?" Full-time island residents were given a special number to get a discount on their groceries, a practice that existed before and after the pandemic. It seemed fair, given the high cost of living on the island. But when the clerk asked the question, I knew the energy around me was about to shift. I was about to identify myself as an outsider, a threat, someone who could have brought the virus with them to the island. I said "no" as quietly as I could, or just shook my head.

During one visit to the store, as I stood in the baking aisle near the flours and sugars, I saw a woman walking toward me the wrong way, against the arrows. I felt immediately threatened by her breaking the rule, by her proximity. I looked at her, at her light blue eyes between her mask and baseball cap, and realized I knew her. She was not a part of our club; her house was in Aquinnah, the beachy town on the tip of the island, but we'd been friends when our kids were little, before she moved to Boston. I said her name and she stopped next to me.

She said, "Oh my God! You're here! How are you?"

Gripping my cart, I said, "I'm not good." I paused and took a breath through my mask. "James left me. He is having an affair." It was the first time I'd told someone in person.

Her eyes widened.

I continued, "I had no idea. I thought I was happily married."

Her eyes started to water, like she was going to cry. She said, "That fucking asshole." It was exactly the right thing to say.

We talked about our kids and the pandemic, about living on the island. We moved to the side of the aisle when someone wanted to pass us. She told me she was volunteering at an island food bank every Friday. She asked if I wanted to come. I said yes. I didn't feel altruistic; at that moment, in April, I could not access the instinct to help anyone. I just liked the idea of busy, straightforward work. Something that would fill a few hours, with someone I knew.

I met her at the food bank every Friday through the spring and summer. It operated out of a church basement in Vineyard Haven. Side by side with other volunteers, I filled bags with cereal boxes, loaves of bread, jars of soup. I counted cucumbers, oranges, bananas, heads of broccoli. I reached into freezers for bags of frozen meatballs, packs of icy salmon. The room was nearly silent as we moved around one another, all intent on finishing our tasks before the end of the shift. It felt, almost immediately, like relief, a pause in my reality, a moment when my brain could rest.

———

In the evenings, after the sun set, once I cleaned up dinner and the girls disappeared to their rooms, I had another expanse of time to fill. If I got in bed before 10 p.m., the night was unbearably long. I continued to rely on jigsaw puzzles, returning to the card table in the living room with a cup of tea, always in the same seat, methodically putting the pieces into place until the clock showed me some mercy, turning to the hour when I could end the day.

As I sat working, I often felt the presence of several of my "deads," as Susan called them—my grandmother, my father, and Lynn, all sitting at the table with me. My grandmother, Babe, was to my left, my father across from me, and Lynn to my right. The feeling was strange; I have never believed in ghosts. But their presence was comforting. It felt like they were standing guard, protecting me.

Next to me, my grandmother's presence was warm, caretaking. Despite (or maybe because of) her failings as a mother, she had been a wonderful grandmother. She loved having me, my brother, and my older cousins at Kiluna Farm. She let us run wild, delighting in our presence, giving us her rapt attention. She insisted we join the adults at cocktails in the library, lunches in her garden, dinners in the dining room. To entertain us, she would arrange a large piece of lettuce or spinach in her teeth, smiling, pretending it wasn't there. We would dissolve into laughter, squealing, "Baba!," the name we called her, the name my children call my mother now. She cheered when my older cousin directed us in elaborate skits, performed for her guests after dinner.

She was tactile and affectionate. She always pulled me onto her lap, kissed the nape of my neck, and told me what flavor she tasted—honey, marmalade, lavender. We played pattycake and backgammon. At bedtime, she used her long, red manicured nails to compose imaginary paintings on my face. She let me try on her jewelry, the two of us in front of her mirror, her graceful hands clasping necklaces around my neck, bracelets on my small wrists. She had fake versions of my favorite pieces made for me for Christmas, all perfectly arranged in a red lacquer box.

My grandmother was, and is, famous for her beauty and style. She was widely photographed, first as a model, then as a young woman in New York, then as a wife, first to my grandfather, Stanley Mortimer, then to Bill Paley. Images of her have become iconic—her face in profile by Richard Avedon; a Horst portrait of her wearing a color-blocked dress, her wrists wrapped in pearls; a series by Slim Aarons at her house in Jamaica, casual in pants and a straw hat. She was meticulous in crafting her image, in how she presented herself to the world—her clothing, her hair and makeup, her jewelry, her homes, how she entertained. She cared about every detail. But her style was also natural, instinctual. It came easily. She set trends by the simplest action, like, famously, tying her scarf to the handle of her pocketbook. She was first named to the International Best Dressed List in 1945, and photographs of her are still printed, posted, and exchanged eighty years later, as new generations adopt her as a fashion icon.

But my grandmother was more than her famous image. She was brilliant, able to lead a conversation on any topic. She was funny. She read constantly. She was rarely at rest. She was an artist, drawing in pencil and sculpting in clay, skills she kept hidden from most of the world. Her father, Harvey Cushing, was a brain surgeon, and I think she inherited her intellect from him, along with her long, elegant hands. Her style was born from the same things—intelligence and artistry.

In a more modern era, she might have claimed her talents publicly, as an editor, a designer, an artist. But she was raised to be a wife, to support her husband, to be the perfect hostess, not to forge an identity apart from those tasks. Within these restrictions, she expressed herself in surfaces.

She died of lung cancer in 1978, the day after her sixty-third birthday, when I was nine. I had not thought of her often in my adult life, usually only if I saw a photograph of her on Instagram, or when my brother and I reminisced about our time at Kiluna Farm. But she was very present in the days, weeks, and months after James left. I often woke up thinking about her, as though she'd been whispering in my ear as I slept.

There were, and are, persistent rumors that her husband, Bill Paley, was a philanderer, rumors fictionalized and retold, in print and on television, like a game of telephone, the facts becoming murkier in each retelling. The rumors are now tied closely with the writer Truman Capote, who was, for a time, my grandmother's close friend and confidant. In 1975, he published a short story in which a man, closely resembling Bill, has an affair with a governor's wife. My grandmother was devastated by the publication of the story, presumably because Truman had betrayed her trust and her privacy, which she guarded fiercely, and co-opted her life for his own purposes. She never spoke to Capote again.

While my mother knew nothing of her stepfather's affairs, she grew to accept that he was unfaithful. It was a common phenomenon among rich and powerful men of the era, part of the package. My mother loved him anyway, as did I. We saw him often in the years after my grandmother's death, at his house at Lyford Cay in the Bahamas or in his apartment on Fifth Avenue. He often expressed deep grief over losing my grandmother, and regret for not appreciating her enough.

My mother also had a pattern of loving unfaithful men, including both of her husbands and her beau of three decades, a journalist. She broke up with the journalist several times because of his infidelity, for the final time in 2018.

Without being conscious of it, as a child and a young adult, I absorbed this legacy of infidelity. I heard my grandfather described as "naughty," my mother's boyfriend as a "flirt," the betrayals chalked up to unavoidable temptation, a natural accessory to success. I saw that my grandmother and mother had forgiven these men, that they'd quietly cleaned up the mess, never saying a word about it. I felt, in my bones, an acceptance of men behaving badly, a value in not calling them out, in protecting a man's belief in his own importance, and a premium placed on keeping such things private.

I thought I had ended this legacy by marrying someone so steady, so unassuming, someone who didn't have a public presence, someone who didn't flirt with other women, at least not in front of me. But I had repeated it in a spectacular fashion. Unlike my grandfather and my mother's boyfriend, James seemed to have no regret, and he didn't want me back. The similarity was that he felt entitled to do it, and he expected me to stay quiet about it.

In the living room each night, as I worked on my puzzle, with my grandmother's ghost sitting calmly beside me, I'd wonder, *What is it about the women in my family that attracts this kind of betrayal? Will the same thing happen to my girls?*

Did James have his own legacy of men behaving badly, walking out without explanation, of women stoically enduring it?

Did we both have another legacy—of adults remaining silent, never explaining what had happened, pushing it underground, into the subconscious lives of the next generations, creating a destiny where the bad thing could be, and would be, repeated?

Lynn, sitting to my right at the card table, looked as she did before she became sick—beautiful with dark, curly hair, a spark in her blue eyes. She could be very blunt and told me once, early in my marriage, that she didn't understand James, she couldn't connect with him, which I took to mean that she didn't like him. I was defensive. But I asked myself now, *Had she identified something I didn't want to see—a coldness, an unknowability?*

Now, in my distress, she wasn't gloating. She seemed to be reminding me of what we'd discussed many times, *Everyone has something. This is yours.* Each life has a defining crisis. This was, of course, an easy one, relative to many, relative to hers.

My father's presence, across from me, was intense. He was upset. It felt like he was saying, *I trusted him too. I trusted him with you.*

———

During the long days of April, while I was falling apart, I had to turn my attention to an immigration case. My law partner and I had a virtual hearing in Queens Family Court scheduled for April 28. Our client, age fourteen, was applying for status as "special immigrant juvenile," a designation that would give her standing to apply for a green card and eventually citizenship. She would need to prove a set of facts, including that her father had abandoned her at birth, that she'd arrived in the United States alone, joining her mother, and that returning to her home country would not be in her best interest. A family court judge would rule on her status; if it was denied, she could face deportation. We were assigned a judge who was, by reputation, the toughest in the building.

We had complicated documents to prepare and file in advance of the hearing—affidavits, a memorandum of law, stipulations, and affirmations. We would need to schedule several Zoom calls with our client and her mother to gather enough information for the affidavits, and to make the case for special immigrant status. We had to get their signatures by mail and enlist a virtual notary.

I would have been able to manage all of this with ease before James's departure, but now, in my ruptured state, it felt impossible. I was unable to read, to write the simplest email, to have a conversation with someone without bursting into tears. I wasn't eating or sleeping much and it showed—every nerve ending felt raw, hypersensitive. I made many mistakes in the affidavits, which my partner caught and fixed. I had a breakdown over scanning and inserting signature pages into documents, a task that felt like the most difficult thing ever required of a person. I was so emotional during one call, my voice catching several times, tears threatening, I had to hang up.

Our client's mother texted me on WhatsApp, "Are you okay, Belle?"

I wrote back, "I'm so sorry, I have a personal issue, something going on in my family."

She responded, "I could tell. I recognize your pain because I have experienced it myself. I am sorry you are suffering. I am praying for you." Our stories were not comparable; my challenges were mild compared to what she had survived. I felt ridiculous. But she didn't seem to see it this way. She offered me empathy. Sitting at my desk, reading her text, I felt overcome with gratitude, for the kindness extended by a woman I barely knew.

As my partner and I pieced things together, slowly revising drafts, rescanning pages, tweaking language, I became more stable and started to rely on the work as I had my walks. It gave form to my day: an hour early in the morning, a few hours after lunch, sitting at my desk, at my computer, refilling the paper tray in the printer. I had a small sense of accomplishment when we finished something, and it oriented me, placing my feet somewhere solid, where I knew what the rules were.

———

In the first weeks after James left, I parked my worry about what would happen to me financially in a corner of my mind. He said we would continue the "status quo," meaning our regular system of funding our accounts, paying bills. He had contributed his standard amount to our checking account on April 1. I thought, *At least I don't have to worry about this. He will not abandon me financially.*

But the signed prenup glowed like a burning ember in my inbox. Before James's lawyer found it in document storage, I had started to believe it was lost. I thought, *Maybe we never signed it? Or maybe we signed it but failed to deliver it back to our lawyers and lost it in the move to Broadway?* Or, in my new mystical moments, *Maybe my father had somehow, from beyond the grave, gotten rid of it?*

The prenup would entitle James to an equal share of everything we had put in joint name, including the house and the apartment. It would allow him to keep everything he earned during the marriage and kept in his own name, a number I did not yet know. This was the change we had made to the prenup in the days before we got married, the change James had requested.

When I found James searching the basement, I knew he wouldn't find the prenup. I had already opened every box, both the ones on the shelves and a bigger set in the crawl space—boxes marked with James's initials, sealed shut with packing tape. I used a box cutter to open each one and pulled out piles of papers, going through every page as I sat cross-legged on the cold concrete floor, the space lit by a single hanging lightbulb. I placed the papers back in their folders, back in the boxes, carefully, neatly, and resealed them with tape so he wouldn't know I'd opened them. After six hours, I came out of the basement covered in dirt, dust, and sweat.

I didn't find it. If I had, I would have burned it.

———

In late April, another friend appeared on the island. She and her husband arrived from overseas. He was an official in the State Department; she worked with refugees. They had lived all over the world and returned to the Vineyard every summer. We didn't know each other well, but our sons were close friends. Her son often slept on our trundle bed, Finn on her sunporch.

After they'd quarantined and tested, she asked me if I wanted to go for a walk. I said, "Yes. I have a story to tell you."

We met in front of her house and started walking up Main Street. It was still cold, with a raw wind, so we were bundled up in puffy coats and hats, our hands in our pockets. I told her what had happened, for the first time unspooling it as a story—the roast chicken, the missed voicemail, the suicide attempt, the exit at dawn. At every dramatic moment, she stopped walking, stunned. She said, "I never would have expected this of James. He seemed so straitlaced. He seemed so devoted to you."

She brought her husband over one day, at his request. We knew each other, having chatted once on a ferry from the Vineyard to Hyannis, but we were not friends. I wasn't sure what to expect. We sat in the living room, separated by the wide coffee table, husband and wife sitting side by side. We removed our masks. The husband was wearing wire-rimmed glasses, a green sweater, jeans. He took a sip of the tea I'd given him and put it down on the table. He cleared his throat.

He said, "I see you walking. I can see how you are suffering. I can see how you are losing weight. You are in 'fight or flight' mode. Your mind is looking for danger, ready to flee. This is a trauma response." He was speaking slowly, like he was choosing each word carefully. I started to cry. He told me how he had descended into a depression the year before. He spoke about what that felt like. He talked about what had helped him—medication, therapy, exercise.

He leaned forward and raised both his hands, his palms facing me. He said, "I want you to understand that what James is doing is *wrong*. The way he left you without explanation is *wrong*. Walking out on his family during a global pandemic is *wrong*. The way he is treating you now is *wrong*. If he tells you it isn't, if anyone tells you it isn't, don't believe them."

He pointed to the driveway behind him. "And if he tries to come back here, you need to padlock the gate."

I slumped in my chair, relieved, for a moment, of what I'd been carrying. This man held it for me as he sat across from me, saying the truth.

———

In the evenings, I taught Evie to drive. It was illegal, she was too young for a learner's permit, but it felt safe on the empty roads. She was determined to master it, to become as competent in driving as she had in cooking, a quest for self-sufficiency in the quiet of those days, when her parents stopped being reliable caretakers. I embraced her growing confidence. It made me feel safe, like everything would be okay, even though she was only fifteen.

We'd get in the car after dinner, Carrie in the back seat, me in front. Evie would drive up and down Franklin Street, passing the house where I'd lived with my six friends during college, down the golf club's dirt road, around the loop of the empty club, and sometimes, when we were feeling brave, through town. We'd often see the sun set over the water as she drove, a few minutes later each night. The girls would play their Spotify mixes on the car stereo. Sometimes we would pass the couple from overseas in their car, going the opposite direction, their son in the driver's seat, doing the same thing.

———

On April 24, my law partner and I filed our client's petition and supporting documents for special immigrant juvenile status. Four days later, we received an email from the judge granting the petition "on submission," meaning that she was ruling on the papers we'd filed; we didn't need to present testimony or appear virtually. The pandemic may have helped us—the court's dockets were overwhelmed. With the order in hand, we could submit our client's paperwork to US Citizenship and Immigration Services for a green card and work permit.

I credit our client, her mother, and my partner for the result, not myself, given the mess that I was then. But I saw that the work—the intense detail of our tasks, the concreteness of writing legal arguments, the creativity required to tell our client's story effectively, the preparation for testimony in court—could be a way forward for me. When I worked, I didn't think about James at all.

———

As the calendar turned to May, the island remained chilly, with temperatures in the fifties, but it also turned green— a crazy, bright kelly green. Trees and lawns all transformed into the vibrant hue. Flowers finally started to bloom. Lily of the valley, my birth flower, sprouted in bunches along Main Street and on the edge of our lawn. Magnolia trees exploded with blossoms in yards on the way to town.

I watched the ospreys carefully. If I stood on the deck outside our kitchen, I could see the nest from above, but it was several hundred yards away; I couldn't see what was inside. James had multiple binoculars for just this purpose, but I had packed them up, along with his clothes from our shared closet, and put it all in boxes in our garage. It hurt to encounter even a single item that belonged to him.

Every day, I leaned over the deck outside our kitchen, squinted, and tried to see if there were any changes in the nest. Soon I noticed that the female was sitting upright throughout the day, her figure low in the nest. The male carried twigs and long pieces of string in his claws, sailing above us, landing on the nest to deliver his treasure. Both the female's posture and the male's activity indicated the very thing I'd hoped for: eggs.

This time I did not think, *I need to tell James*. I thought, *He's going to miss this. He's going to miss everything.*

———

On my birthday, May 6, the girls made me dinner: spaghetti carbonara, arugula salad with pine nuts and parmesan, devil's food cake with white icing. They served it on my grand-parents' flowered china, at the table on our screened porch, with votive candles and vases of flowers—perfect pink peonies that arrived in a box from my mother and wild island flowers from Susan, delivered that morning by our beloved former babysitter. She had worked for us for ten years, starting when she was sixteen and Evie was two. She was now married and had three kids of her own. When she dropped off the flowers, she and her daughter stood ten feet from our door, blowing us kisses. She had been rattled by the news of James leaving. She said that during the summers she spent in our house, she had thought of us as a perfect family.

We wore our nicest dresses that night, our fanciest sandals. It was the first time I'd felt hungry. I ate everything they gave me. I ached, though, as I sat there, blowing out my birthday candles, carefully placed by the girls in the cake, five on one side, one on the other, for fifty-one. It was the first marking of time without James. He had sent a text in the morning, the first I'd received in weeks. It said, "Happy Birthday!" The casualness of the exclamation mark, the enthusiasm, felt worse than saying nothing at all.

I got the same text from James's sister and mother, individually: "Happy Birthday!" Two words, after almost two months of silence. His brother's text was a little bit longer, "No matter what happens, we love you!" An exclamation mark again. No acknowledgment of having cut me off, of their brother's continued absence, of my children's heart-break.

Is this how they did things? Pretend nothing happened, let enough time go by, be cheerful, and all will be well? Were they afraid too

many words would awaken my upset, would call out their abandon-
ment, would become too much?

I didn't reply.

James had never cared much about birthdays. In his family, they exchanged only small items, usually a book, perhaps
because they could not afford more than that. My family was
the opposite. My mother said it was the only day her own
mother paid attention to her, so birthdays—hers in January, mine in May, my brother's in August—were days we
really celebrated. My father and Susan were the same way. At
both houses, we were given breakfast in bed, a pile of presents, a celebratory dinner. I did this for my kids too, serving
them pancakes or Fruity Pebbles or Dunkin' Donuts on the
same raised tray every year, a pyramid of presents next to
them, usually one big surprise—an electric piano when Evie
turned ten, cell phones when they turned twelve, a coveted
jersey, or the newest American Girl doll. They had parties
with themes, cakes shaped like a Candy Land board, a pirate
ship, Dora the Explorer. James didn't understand our enthusiasm for birthdays and didn't know how to do it for me. He
usually bought me a gift card, at my request, and I had to
remind him to make a reservation for dinner, to get me my
favorite chocolate cake from William Greenberg. Over the
years, I stopped asking him to make plans; I orchestrated the
day for myself, I went to the movies, I made dinner reservations, Susan bought me the cake. It didn't really bother me. I
saw it as a difference in how we grew up, not a reflection of
how he felt about me.

In 2016, he surprised me. The morning of my forty-
seventh birthday, with the kids around us, he handed me a

small box wrapped with a ribbon. Inside was a single key. On the Vineyard, most beaches are private, and access to them is a form of real estate. Families pass beach keys down over generations, and others sell them on the open market for great sums. The key in the box was to Black Point, one of the most beautiful beaches on the island. We'd been renting a key from an owner for a few years. I took the kids as often as I could, even on cloudy days. It took us half an hour to get there—twenty minutes to Chilmark, then ten minutes on a dirt road marked only by a long row of mailboxes. We'd carry our bags and our boogie boards, our chairs, our paper bags of sandwiches, down the boardwalk, over the dunes to the big reveal—the Atlantic Ocean, miles of beach, all of it quiet and peaceful. When they were little, the kids often fell asleep in the car on the way home, leaning like dominoes against one another in their sandy bathing suits. Or we sang with the radio and picked up flatbread pizzas from a restaurant near the airport, eating slices in the car, grease dripping on our bare thighs. James was never a fan of beaches, but the kids and I loved it. Owning a key seemed like an impossibility, but there it was, on my birthday, gleaming in my hand.

———

My neighbor in New York texted me in mid-May: "I'm worried. James is throwing away so much stuff." She had found at least a dozen black garbage bags in our floor's shared refuse room, all filled and tied.

My neighbor and I had known each other for almost eighteen years, having moved onto the twenty-fifth floor at the same time, when the building first opened. She was older than

I was, with three grown children. She was kind and warm and I often sought her out for advice, especially about parenting. She and her husband had never complained during the many years my kids ran up and down our shared hallway, screaming, kicking hard soccer balls against their door.

I had told her about James's affair, about him leaving. She groaned and said, "He thinks he's original, but he's not." She said she'd seen it many times before, the exit of a middle-aged man for a younger woman. She noted that he'd left me the year I turned fifty, the ultimate cliché.

When I pictured the garbage bags, I thought of James's apartment on White Street, the one he'd shared with Mark, the spareness, the lack of things on his side. I thought, *He's returning to that person, the guy without stuff.* As he took flight from us, he was getting rid of everything that weighed him down.

I'd discovered he'd taken his collection of Rolex watches from the Vineyard the day of the turkey sandwich, probably filling the duffel bag at the last moment so I wouldn't see it. There had been a dozen of them, in light green boxes, stacked in a drawer in our bedroom. I learned later that he sold all but one, the Daytona I had given him as a wedding present. It was engraved with the date, 6/5/99. I don't know if he kept it out of sentiment or if the engraving made it less marketable. I hoped it was the former but suspected the latter.

Eventually, he also gave away his motorcycles. He sold his vintage boat. When he came to collect his boxes in the garage, he threw most of his clothes away. He told me he didn't want any of our wine, even the bottles he'd bought.

He had accumulated these things over twenty years—

adding, building, creating a life with all of it. They were the spoils of his success, markers of how far he had come, from the boy whose parents had lost everything, who couldn't buy anything. And now he was dismantling it, like he was dismantling our family, taking off the costume of husband, father, owner as quickly as he'd put it on. He was shedding.

But what was he becoming? The teenage rebel he'd been, the spirit of Mark, willing to burn it all down? A hedge fund bachelor? A husband to a younger wife, starting again? I didn't know.

I wrote to my neighbor, "Don't worry, it's not my stuff. It's his."

———

I had never been in regular therapy. I tried a few times, once during college and once after my father died, but I hated it, the pressure to talk, to analyze myself, especially when the therapist was mostly silent. To me, as a shy person, therapy felt like torture.

After James left, during the weeks I couldn't move from bed, my mother and Susan insisted I talk to someone. Susan found a psychiatrist who made room for me. We talked on the phone twice a week. I closed my door to take her calls in the late afternoon, always on the phone for some reason, never on Zoom. I could picture her any way I wanted to, so I imagined Nora Ephron.

She asked questions, she reacted. I didn't have silences to fill. She was blunt and, like the husband from overseas, she offered clear opinions.

It was wrong to leave a marriage with no warning and no explanation.

It was highly unusual not to want custody of kids who were as young as twelve.

It wasn't normal to search the basement for a prenup after telling children about a divorce.

While James failed to acknowledge what was happening, the psychiatrist made my reality clear. I could tell myself, at least until it became fuzzy again, *This is not okay.*

———

The third week in May, I decided to take the girls back to New York for a few days. They had orthodontist appointments that, to Evie, felt urgent—missing an appointment would delay her most fervent wish, the removal of her braces. And we needed to pick up our dog—our eight-year-old Goldendoodle. The boarder had picked him up from our apartment in mid-March, when we thought we were going on vacation for spring break. We all missed him.

I also wanted the girls to see James. I was determined to keep a tether between them, even as he was walking away. And maybe I would discover something, a clue about why he had left, about what he was doing now. Massachusetts and New York were still in lockdown, and COVID cases were raging in Manhattan, but it didn't dissuade me. I put the girls in the Toyota and we boarded the ferry.

During that time in the pandemic, I-95 was an eerily open road; we made the trip in less than four hours. When we pulled up in front of our building on Broadway, James was standing outside. I'd asked him to be there, to greet the girls and spend time with them. The sight of him still made my heart leap. I thought, *There's my husband.* And then, quickly, *No, this man is not him.*

As he welcomed the girls, with the same blue mask and excited energy we'd seen in April, I thought, *Will he notice that my clothes are hanging off me? Will he be worried?* But he didn't look at me at all.

He took the girls up to the apartment, and I went for a walk to give them time alone. I headed west to the Hudson River. When I got to the esplanade, I stopped, trying to decide whether to walk north or south. It was disorienting to be back there, with so many people, after two months on our quiet island. I turned north and started walking, passing familiar landmarks, the playground at North Moore Street, the kayaks at Pier 26, the I WANT TO THANK YOU mural on Pier 40.

I worried for the girls, now in the apartment with James. His visible happiness was so incongruous with what he had left behind, with what I thought of as emotional wreckage, like the aftermath of a hurricane. I didn't know how he would act with them now, a month after he'd broken the news. *Would he apologize to them for leaving, for breaking up our family, for the affair? Or would he continue to act like nothing was wrong?*

Once I reached Houston Street, I turned around and retraced my steps, south on the West Side Highway, east on Chambers Street, walking slowly to give them more time, but fast enough to meet the boarder's van, arriving soon. As I crossed Church Street, I saw James walking in the opposite direction, toward me. I stopped and stood at the edge of the sidewalk as he approached, not sure of what he would say, what we would say to each other. It was the first time we'd been alone

together since the scene in the basement. He looked in my direction, but his gaze was aimed somewhere above my head.

He kept walking, not pausing, and smiled broadly. As he
passed, he said, "They are great! Everything is great!"

I stood there for several minutes, watching him cross the
street. I almost yelled, *"What the fuck are you talking about?"*
but I knew he would make me feel like I was crazy to be
upset, crazy to think the girls *weren't* fine, that anything
about the scenario was wrong. I couldn't bear that conversation. So I said nothing.

I met the boarder's van on Broadway. James was allergic
to pugs, so we'd looked for a more hypoallergenic breed. He
also wanted a bigger dog; he said he would feel silly walking
anything small. On a friend's recommendation, we picked a
Goldendoodle and named him Charlie Blue. When I walked
our new puppy around our neighborhood, people stopped
me and said, "Look at those paws! He's going to be *huge!*"

I protested, "No, no, the breeder said he will only be
thirty pounds, fifty at most."

And then, like Clifford the Big Red Dog, Charlie grew
before our eyes to almost a hundred pounds, with a thick
fluffy coat. He looked more like a horse than a dog. When he
turned one, he suddenly became reactive to other dogs. On
walks, he barked, snarled, lunged, trying to protect us. At
our boarder's urging, I took him to the veterinary hospital
at the University of Pennsylvania for an evaluation. He was
diagnosed with generalized anxiety disorder and put on a
high dose of fluoxetine (Prozac). But it didn't help; he was
still reactive. He could go outside only early in the morning
and late at night, when it was less crowded, and even then it

was a terrifying game of avoiding other dogs, scanning the street to find a safe path. I found it so scary, I begged James to walk him after he got home from work, while I washed dishes and put the kids to bed. He did it, but he always complained about it, having to go out after dinner, into the cold.

As Charlie jumped down from the van, his tail wagging, I thought, *Maybe this is why James left? Because he hated walking the dog?*

Charlie pulled me into the building, racing down the lobby floor to the elevator, slipping side to side on the polished marble. When I let him into the apartment, the girls screamed in delight. They threw themselves on the floor to hug him. They kissed his nose and fed him stale biscuits from the kitchen cabinet. It felt like the first time I'd seen them smile in weeks. We ended up on Carrie's bed, the dog stretched between the girls, each of them cuddling the length of him, rubbing his pink stomach. I lay at his feet, resting my head on his thigh, taking in his dog smell, the warmth of him.

I asked, "How did it go with Dad?"

They answered, almost in unison, "Weird."

I knew I had to abide by the most sacred rule of divorce: do not badmouth the other parent. I'd hated it when my parents spoke meanly about each other; even the slightest unkindness upset me. But, as I looked at the girls, I knew they needed some acknowledgment of what was happening, of how strange it was. Being fake with them, or lying, felt unbearable.

I groped for the right words, speaking slowly: "You're right, this is weird. Your dad is going through something. I don't know what it is. But you aren't wrong to feel like it's strange."

They were quiet for a minute. Evie said, "Yeah, it's like he's a different person."

Carrie asked, "Does he still have that girlfriend?" She said the fruit name.

I answered, "I don't know." I didn't.

Evie asked, "Is he having a midlife crisis?"

What was happening seemed stranger than a midlife crisis—something more than buying a sports car or having an affair—but it was an explanation my girls could hang on to, one that was about him, not them.

I said, "I think so, something like that."

They were quiet again.

I said, "He loves you guys so much. I know that for sure." It felt important to say this. His love for them was an uncomplicated fact. It was something else that was missing—care, worry, heartache.

Carrie looked at the dog. "He loves you too, Chuckie. He's going to be so happy to see you."

I wondered, for a moment, *Maybe the dog will be the thing that wakes him up? Maybe the dog will make him miss us?* But at the same time, I knew, *He's not going to care. He's going to leave me with this responsibility too. I will have to walk the dog every day until he dies.*

The girls slept in my bed that night, the dog on the floor next to us, all of them snoring softly.

———

I barely slept while we were in the city. I lay between the girls in my marital bed, wide awake. James had bought the mattress four months earlier, in January 2020. It was a wildly expensive Sleep Number bed. He was elated about it. He preferred a bed that was pillow soft; I preferred hard as a rock. The Sleep Number allowed each of us to pick our desired firmness using a remote control. James enlisted four men who worked in the building to help install the mattress in the frame of our upholstered bed, a task that took several hours. We laughed that night as we played with the numbers, as we lifted and lowered the head and foot of the mattress, like a hospital bed, as if we were suddenly eighty.

What was he thinking then, as we laughed together? Was he already having the affair? Did he know he was going to leave me two months later? Why would he buy such an expensive bed, one clearly designed for two people to share?

I got up, climbing over Evie in the dark, feeling frantic, suddenly, to find something, anything to explain his exit, his betrayal, evidence of a gathering storm, clouds I hadn't seen, a puzzle piece. *What had I missed?*

I looked through our bedside tables, opening the drawers slowly, softly, so I wouldn't wake the girls, using the light on my phone to see inside. I found only phone chargers and socks in his drawers, loose change and hair elastics in mine. I looked through his desk, which sat between our closets. It was nearly bare—only a stapler, black binder clips, a few unused gift cards, his favorite black mechanical pencils from Davis Polk, the kids' passports placed neatly in the corner of one drawer. The stacks of papers he usually kept on top of his desk and on the windowsills were gone. He must have thrown them away, in the black garbage bags my neighbor had found.

I looked in our shared closets and shelves, at his suits and shirts packaged by the dry cleaner. I loved his clothes, the way he dressed for work—a navy or charcoal-gray suit, a crisp shirt, a tie with some color—what he'd worn when we met, the attire of a responsible and trustworthy man, leaving each day to make a living for his family. I longed for the way it felt to hug him in his suit, how it felt only two months before, when he left for the office, his hair still wet from the shower, his cheek still cold and soft from shaving, kissing me goodbye.

His wardrobe looked lighter, culled. There were fewer sweaters, fewer T-shirts, fewer suits.

I continued my search in our bathroom. We had separate sinks on either side of a square, glass shower. I opened his drawers and saw his razors, his shaving cream, the black drugstore combs he used to part his hair, several boxes of Nicorette. He'd quit smoking when Evie was born, giving up the two cigarettes he had every evening, and he used the gum to curb nicotine cravings. I'd often found his chewed pieces around the apartment, the gum placed back in its wrapper, left on windowsills and countertops.

I opened his medicine cabinet. It was full, brimming with the things he used regularly: Band-Aids, Tums, aspirin, deodorant, and a row of bottles from our local drugstore. I took down each vial of pills, looking at the dates. There were old antibiotics, newer prescriptions, dates ranging from ten years ago to the prior month.

My heart raced, thinking, somehow, the pills would provide an answer, a story that made sense. One that did not involve a wholesale rejection of me. One that probably felt familiar to me—the big reveal of my father's amber bottles. I counted the pills, trying to calculate if he had stopped taking something, or started something new. But there was nothing I could hang my hat on, no clear explanation, only my face in the mirror, loose pills in my hand.

I thought, *What am I doing?*

Being a detective, searching for answers, was seductive—the thrill of the hunt, the discovery of a smoking gun, the mystery solved. But it also felt awful, the desperation of it, the ultimate lack of answers, like getting mired in a swamp, one that was going to pull me under. I had to get out of this place—a place that was all about him, all about the woman he was seeing, all about trying to understand how or why this had happened.

Susan had given me a trick she used with her patients in therapy. She said, "Imagine yourself on a theater stage with James. Whenever the spotlight is on him, move it to you, so that you are lit, and he is in the dark." It often worked, for a moment. I was able to pause the obsessive thoughts, about him, about the affair, about why he had left me.

Feeling gutted and exhausted, I closed the medicine cabinet and went back to the bedroom, groping my way in the dark. I climbed into bed with the girls, gently rolling Carrie to the middle of the mattress.

———

James told me he was splitting his time between our apartment and the Beekman Street apartment he'd bought for his mother and stepfather in 2018. A second apartment should have been a clear sign of infidelity—it would have been easy for him to meet other women there when his mother and stepfather were away. But I didn't think it was the site of his betrayal. I had keys to the apartment, and it was filled with his parents' things—their flannel sheets, their books by the bed, their vanilla yogurt in the fridge—the unsexy belongings of a couple in their eighties. I think he was more likely to go to hotels, including the new, chic Beekman Hotel next door. This is what I imagined when I pictured James and the woman together, the awful images of their coupling.

He also told me, by text, that he'd signed a contract to buy a two-bedroom apartment in a building on Park Row, one of the new high-rises that had replaced J&R Music World. The news was startling. The apartment wasn't a rental; he was buying it. He was committing to a life away from us.

I looked at the sales website for the building, at the model two-bedroom floor plan and photos. It looked modern and expensive. *But a two-bedroom? Would he be able to fit all three kids in one bedroom?* I still thought he would want to make a home for them, that he wouldn't follow through with his decision to have no custody, no overnights. Even if he refused formal custody, I thought the kids would stay with him now and then, that Carrie would go there after school when she chose to, that she would have a room to sleep in, that he would give her a key.

———

Our second night in New York, James brought sushi for the girls for dinner. We sat in our usual places at our kitchen table, James next to Evie, me next to Carrie, Finn's chair empty. The girls were silent as they ate their favorite popcorn shrimp and spicy tuna rolls.

James seemed jubilant. He said, "Evie, how are the geese? Have you kept them away?"

"Yes," she said with certainty.

There were dozens of geese on the lawn every day. It was covered in goose shit.

James turned to Carrie. "How is your tennis game? You are so good at tennis!"

Carrie answered quietly, "It's okay."

I felt unable to help the conversation along. My body was like lead again, as it had been in the first weeks. It was hard to even raise my arm. We were sitting at the table where we'd had so many family meals. Where we'd sat as recently as March, unaware that everything was about to change, in the world and in our family. I could almost see the dark cloud hovering over us. But it was as though the cloud, the darkness, was only over me and the girls; James sat under a sunny sky.

———

The next day, when I brought the girls back from the orthodontist, we found James in the living room, lying on a mat on the floor, doing crunches. He was fully clothed, in corduroys and a button-down shirt, wearing sneakers. His trainer was on an iPad, the screen leaning against the back of one of my grandparents' wooden hall chairs. I'd never seen James work out with a trainer before. He looked energized, sweating with the effort. He had always been slim, but he looked much fitter, more muscular, his shoulders and biceps visible beneath his shirt. I felt a familiar tug of desire for him, for his body. I scolded myself, *Stop. He's naked with someone else now.*

I stood over him and said, "What are you doing?"

He answered, mid-crunch, "I'm working out. I can't go to the gym." He sounded irritated.

He could have done the session at his mother's apartment, where he'd spent the night. He could have chosen a time when we weren't there. I think he wanted us to see it. He wanted an audience to his transformation.

The girls and I went to our rooms and shut our doors. I could still hear his trainer directing him. I could still hear him panting.

———

We left for the Hamptons the next day. I was anxious to see Finn. He had moved in with Susan and her quarantine pod—a friend, her nephew (my cousin), and his wife—in Sagaponack. We had decided that we could risk being together since we didn't have any COVID symptoms.

I couldn't take that risk with my mother. Her lungs were prone to infection and any kind of cold took her down for weeks. I worried about her a lot, alone in her house in Bellport. We texted often and FaceTimed once a week during dinner. I'd lean my phone against a vase on our kitchen table so she could chat with us as we ate our meal and she ate hers. In our conversations without the girls, she continued to be fierce in her support of me, in how she felt about James leaving, in her faith that I would survive it.

We walked into Susan's house and collapsed into her, the three of us in her arms. Finn came down the stairs and we jumped on him, clutching his shoulders, his waist. He seemed to have grown several inches since March. His short hair, thick like mine, had grown out over his ears.

On the phone and over FaceTime, Finn had been reluctant to talk to me about the divorce. And I struggled with what to say to him. I didn't want to force a conversation he wasn't ready for. And I didn't want him to worry about me. Since he was little, he'd been hypersensitive to other people's feelings and moods, especially mine. Whenever I felt any shift in emotion, he would ask, "Are you okay, Mommy?" So, when we spoke that spring, I tried to be cheerful, to stay on happy topics—the dog, cooking, his friends.

I hugged his long, lean frame. He had just turned eighteen. His birthday was two days before mine. For the first time in his life, I hadn't been with him to celebrate. He was taller than me now, but still more boy than man, his cheeks round, his skin soft.

I looked up at him. "I missed you so much," I said.

"Me too, Mama," he replied.

I thought, *How will I do this? How will I guide him to adulthood, to college and employment and life, if James is absent? How will I be kind about his father and, at the same time, teach him that his father's actions—infidelity, silence, absence—are not okay?* It felt impossible.

My cousin, a chef, cooked dinner for all of us and I slept in Susan's king-size bed, the only available spot. She brought me tea and put her cool hand on my forehead, as she had when I was a child.

She said, "I don't know how you are in one piece."

"I'm not sure I am," I answered.

She pulled the covers up around me, tucking me in. "This is harder than being widowed."

Two years after losing my father, Susan met a successful screenwriter. They never married but they were together for twenty years, until his death from cancer in 2018. I thought of her as twice widowed.

I said, "No, it's not. Not at all. I saw what you went through. And my kids still have a father."

She answered, "I know, it is different. But I would not choose this. The hurt, the betrayal, the wondering what was real and what wasn't. The fact that he is still out there, wanting a different life."

I sighed. "I guess it's apples and oranges. Different forms of hell."

It seemed funny in that moment, the way life had turned out for us. We both laughed.

And then I felt the ache again, thinking of James and my father, of both men I had lost.

———

We went back to the Vineyard two days later, failing to convince Finn to come with us. He wanted to stay with his friends, including two of the boys he'd lived with during lockdown. The three of them were working for my cousin's underground catering business, run from Susan's kitchen. They chopped vegetables, packed containers, labeled bags, and loaded them in the car for Susan and her friend to deliver, house to house, all over the Hamptons.

The girls and I took the Cross Sound Ferry from Orient Point on Long Island to New London, Connecticut, then the bigger ferry from Woods Hole to the Vineyard. The dog spent the five-hour trip trying to get into Carrie's lap in the back seat. He panted on her for so long, the front of her T-shirt was completely wet. She alternated between laughing and asking me for help—he weighed more than she did. I stopped several times, on the shoulder of the highway, to push him to the other side of the seat.

———

As June started, the air warmed, the days lengthened. The lake became more active. Boats appeared on moorings. Clammers waded in the shallow water. Kayaks and canoes glided past our house at sunset.

Early one morning, standing on the boardwalk, I saw a different shape in the osprey nest, a small, huddled mass. The mass moved, separating, revealing three tiny heads. I gasped. The eggs had hatched.

After the chicks appeared, the couple became more protective of the nest, squawking loudly if we came too close, circling the perimeter, warning us away. The male became more active in his search for food; it seemed like he was fishing all day long. He flew above us before he dove into the lake; a fast, vertical dive, shifting at the last moment with his legs and head forward. He emerged from the water carrying a small fish, an unmistakable silhouette in the sky. He delivered it to the nest, a gift to the female and their babies, and then flew out again. Hunting and gathering.

I brought the girls to the boardwalk to show them the chicks. As we stood there, their arms around my waist, I thought they might mention their father. But they didn't say anything at all. I took a photo of the nest, the little heads, the two parents guarding them, and texted it to James. I was aware of the not-so-subtle subtext—here was an intact family, here was a father providing for, and protecting, his three offspring and their mother.

James wrote back, "Wow!"

———

As summer started, club members returned to the island, moving into their homes and rentals. They quarantined for two weeks, tested, and then joined the social life, sometimes masked, sometimes not. We considered it a large, safe bubble, and it turned out to be so—there were very few cases of COVID at the club in the summer of 2020. There was no official camp, Sunday barbecue, or weekly lecture series, but groups still gathered, for cocktails and dinners outside, for tennis on the club's courts, for an afternoon swim on the pier.

I dreaded running into people. The pandemic had suspended real life for three months, allowing me to hide, to be cocooned during my most raw weeks, spared the encounters that would have been so difficult, at school pickup, birthday parties, meetings. This was the flip side of my experience— I'd endured James's exit alone, without my family and friends, but also without the daily exposures, without the need to pull myself together, without an audience to witness my falling apart.

I knew that news of James leaving me was already spreading at the club, as juicy gossip does. In my mind, it was the only thing people were talking about, even though we were in the middle of a pandemic, even though every family was stressed. And I felt a deep sense of embarrassment about it. James was the one who had an affair, who walked out, but the shame had become mine. I had made it mine. I was an abandoned wife, a woman rejected by her husband, a woman who had failed to keep her family together. I would be the outsider among all the married people, all the intact families, all the women who were wanted by their husbands.

I had several friends in New York who were divorced, including two high-school classmates whose husbands had affairs and left them. These friends were warm and compassionate, calling often, understanding my anguish in a way others couldn't. There was no one like that on the Vineyard that summer. Everyone in my circle, and almost everyone at the club, was married.

I didn't expect anyone to mention the dissolution of my marriage to me directly. The club was a place where most things appeared perfect, and people rarely shared anything difficult about their lives. This was a summer escape, a vacation, and it was meant to be light. There was also a propriety, a formality to the club, which was different from New York or the Hamptons, different from any place I'd ever been.

I forced myself to do my normal walk, the loop taking me through the club, now populated with members—tennis players, children on the playground, young mothers pushing strollers. I don't know why I made myself do this; it would have been easy to cut through the woods, missing the club entirely. But I told myself I had to face it.

As the temperatures climbed into the seventies, I swapped my jeans and boots for shorts and sneakers, but I always wore a long-sleeved shirt to feel some measure of protection, some armor. I set out in one direction or the other, but always passed through the club's main drag.

When I saw someone I knew, we'd stop to say hello and I'd tell them, "James left me. I'm devastated," or something similar. It didn't matter who it was—a contemporary I knew well or the most formal grandparent. I'm amazed by this now, by my candor, given my embarrassment, given my shyness, but it felt like my only choice. I had an open wound and needed to say, *This is why I am bleeding*. And maybe, even then, I wanted some control over the story. I wanted the truth of what happened to come from my mouth.

When I spoke, people looked surprised, sometimes shocked. It was the story itself but also the fact that I was saying it, someone they thought of as quiet and private. It felt like I was crossing some kind of invisible line, of what they expected of me, of how they believed someone should act when they've been left by their husband of twenty years.

Some people moved toward me, literally closing the gap between us, putting their hands on me. A mother of four, someone I didn't know well, grabbed me by the shoulders, shook her head, and said, definitively, "No. No. That is not right. You are hanging out with me. I'm going to take care of you." Another woman came to find me as I stood awkwardly near the club's inn, waiting to drive the girls home from tennis. She faced me, a few feet apart, her dog on a leash, and said, "I am so sorry. I am so disappointed in James." She shook her head. It felt good, these women looking me straight in the eye, saying what had happened, being clear in how they felt about it.

Others moved away from me, often literally, a few slow steps away from the heat of me. It was the equivalent of New York friends who responded to my news with texts like, "I'll be thinking of you," or "Sending love to you and the kids." These responses, though kind, felt distancing, a turning away when I had flung my doors wide open. I had never thought about this before—how a closed-ended response, no matter how well-intentioned, can feel like an ending—the declining of an invitation to engage.

Still, I asked myself, *Would I have wanted to hear about someone's divorce? Would I have moved toward them? Or would I have assumed it was too private to talk about, or that they were a bit unhinged, and moved away?* I hope I would have chosen the former, but I'm not sure.

And, even then, I knew it was possible that I was responsible for the distance: *In my reserve, my quiet, as a married person, did I fail to plant the seeds, to invest in friendships, to earn the kind of embrace I am looking for now?*

I couldn't predict how people would react, who would move toward me, who would move away. One morning, as I passed the club's inn, I saw a man I knew well, someone I considered a friend. I was about to say hello, smiling and lifting my hand to wave, his name on my tongue, but he turned suddenly and walked in the opposite direction. This happened again at a cocktail party; two men I knew well turned from me as I approached.

I tried to make sense of it with Susan. She urged me to

look at it generously: *Maybe they were proving their loyalty to their wives by not speaking to a newly single woman? Or they had an unconscious fear of contagion, one divorce leading to another? Or, most likely, they just didn't know what to say?*

Susan said, "I think people have a language for death; they know what to do, what to say. But there is no script for divorce, especially one as dramatic as yours."

I tried to hold on to this, fighting against a less generous explanation: *Now that I was no longer a wife, now that I had lost my status, I was no longer worth the effort. These men would save their energy, their loyalty, for the man, the tennis player, the hedge fund guy, whenever he decided to return.*

Another day, on the wide two-way street between town and the club, I saw a man biking in the opposite direction. I waved and expected him to keep going. I didn't know him well; he was married with three kids and famous in the world of professional sports. But he stopped, got off his bike, and walked over to my side of the street, holding the bike by the handlebars. He said, "I want you to know how sorry I am that this happened to you." He asked how I was doing, how the kids were doing. He said, "I don't understand a man leaving his family like that."

I felt each interaction in my body, a joyful lift when someone was warm, when someone acknowledged me and what had happened; a crash when they didn't, when they avoided me. I was inviting all of it, the roller coaster of emotion, almost like I was asking people to declare themselves, in one camp or the other—not between me and James, but between connecting with me or not. As I put on my sneakers each morning, I braced myself, not knowing what would come next.

—

The mother of four invited me over for a glass of wine on her porch, following through with her promise to take care of me. Two women joined us, one I knew well, one I didn't know at all. The latter was tall, brunette. When she sat down, she said, "God, when you don't have a husband here, no one invites you to anything!" Her husband was at home in Connecticut, soon to arrive.

Once seated, she told us how difficult her sister's divorce was. It was a similar fact pattern, the husband leaving for someone else. She said, "I still miss my brother-in-law. He was so much fun." She looked at me, narrowed her eyes, and said, "I love James. He's the *best*."

I don't think she had ever had a conversation with James, at least not a substantive one.

She went on for a long time, praising her brother-in-law and James in equal measure. I felt so pummeled, so weak, I couldn't get myself to say anything in response, or to stand up and leave. I sat through it all, frozen. The hostess and my other friend didn't say anything either. They told me afterward they didn't know how to stop her.

The next day, I felt like I had taken a bullet in my chest. I could not understand why this woman had framed my story with sympathy toward James and not me, especially so soon after he had left, when I was clearly so fragile.

Again, Susan and I tried to look at it kindly: *She was speaking about her own experience, her own family's experience with a difficult divorce. My story brought up her complicated feelings about it. She felt it was important to defend the person who was absent, whose reputation was being trampled, to remind everyone, including me, of his humanity.*

But to me, in my raw state, it felt like she was offering a blueprint for how the community should think about what happened to me: *James is the injured party, not Belle. He is the prize. He is the one we should keep.*

———

In the heat of late July, the osprey chicks, now juveniles, learned to fly. They were tentative at first, venturing only a yard from the nest, and then, as they gained confidence, soaring farther over the water, over our lawn, their big wings flapping slowly, steadily.

One afternoon, a juvenile landed on our chimney. I thought it was the male parent at first, leaving the nest to give his offspring room to spread their wings. But after five hours, it was clear it was one of the juveniles, successful in its outbound flight but now unable to lift off again. I felt an intense anxiety for the bird, lost and stuck, its tender talons on the hot tiles. I called the osprey experts, asking for a rescue, but they said not to interfere, that the bird would leave once it had burned enough calories to make it easier to fly again. The next morning, the juvenile was gone from the chimney. I counted five heads in the nest. The bird had made it home.

———

I continued to walk, now with company. It was more comfortable for me to talk with friends when we were in motion, side by side, rather than face-to-face. On one walk, through the dirt roads of a neighboring golf club, a friend told me she had gone to a dinner party with a group of couples I knew well. I hadn't been invited. I felt a slight prick of pain from this—*Would I be excluded from these dinners now that I was single?* But I let it go. I sensed she was about to tell me something that would be more painful.

She said that a man at the dinner, someone who was charming and well-liked, had said to the table, "James leaving Belle could be a good thing. My father left my mother for another woman, and she was the love of his life. They were so happy together."

I stopped walking, stunned by her words. *This was a good thing? This was a love story? What about MY love story with James?*

I turned to her. "Why would he say that?"

She said, "I don't think he meant to be unkind. I think he was trying to find the silver lining to all this."

All this. My story. The end of my marriage.

For the second time, my experience had been rewritten, the characters recast, the ending changed. In this man's telling, I was the casualty of someone else's destiny. My despair was their happy ending.

I doubled over, seized with a desperate, wild hurt. I said, "I'm sorry, I have to go."

I turned and ran from my friend, sprinting down the dirt road, a mile to my house, to safety.

———

The club had a rule for the rare divorces—only one spouse could remain a member; the other had to reapply, starting the three-year process from scratch. I wasn't aware of anyone who had reapplied. I assumed that after James and I divorced, I would be the one to stay, acquiring the membership "share" we were given when we joined the club. He would transfer the share to me. It was what made sense: I was taking care of the kids; I had bought our house; I was there.

But in the tender days of July, a friend told me this wasn't clear to everyone. She had heard other members talking about it, discussing whether James or I would—or should—be the surviving member.

We were on my porch, drinking tea in the late afternoon. I was stunned when she reported this.

I asked, "Why?"

She looked down. "What I've heard is that it's not a straightforward situation since you and James arrived at the club together. Usually, it's clear who should stay since the husband or wife grew up here."

It felt like my heart was seizing again, as it had on the dirt road. *I could be cast out?*

I said, "I don't understand. He's in New York. He's having an affair. I'm here with the kids. Why wouldn't it be me?"

I was sure that if the situations were reversed, if I had walked out on my family during a pandemic, if I was having an affair, there would be no conversation about who would remain a member.

My friend nodded. "I agree with you, believe me. I just thought I should tell you. I'm worried."

I wasn't upset with her. I needed to know what I was facing. But it brought me to my knees. It put me back on the bathroom floor, literally. It was only a club, a microcosm of life, but at that moment, during the pandemic, it was my whole world.

I decided that I would never go back to the club. I would hide in my house until I could return to New York. The possibility that I could be rejected because of James's rejection of me did not seem survivable.

But I had a competing feeling, another voice in my head saying, *They expect you to disappear. And if you disappear from here, you might disappear completely.*

I also knew it mattered to the girls that I keep appearing at the club. They were managing the gossip too. One girl had said to Evie, "I heard your dad's girlfriend has little kids." She said it casually, but each word—*girlfriend, little, kids*—was wounding. I don't know where this teenager had heard these details; they were not part of the story I told.

If the girls saw me going to dinner parties, if they saw me standing on a lawn having a cocktail with the other parents, it would all feel less grim, less dire. It would be a clear sign to them that their world wasn't falling apart, at least not this part of their world. So, even in my despair, even knowing that some people didn't expect me to stay, I kept showing up.

Often, when I showed up, when I moved toward people, I was stunned by how kind they could be, how much they opened up in response to my being open, how new friendships formed, how old ones deepened. A new friend invited me over every morning, in the middle of my walk, to drink shots of vitamin C and talk about what I was feeling that day. Another friend cooked for me every week, welcoming me to her table again and again, keeping things light and cheerful. The couple from overseas dropped off my favorite ham and cheese croissants on Saturday mornings. Other friends arrived at night with bags of hot doughnuts from a bakery in Oak Bluffs. Several women walked with me, one always remembering to pause with me at the church on William Street, joining me in my silent prayer. The community looked out for my girls, waving to them as they passed on their bikes. I soaked up each gesture, each connection, as if it were oxygen.

But, at the same time, I learned quickly not to say too much, to censor myself. Several times, when I described what was happening to me, adding detail, I could feel the other person withdraw, looking down. As the words came from my mouth, trying to offer evidence ("He never told me he was unhappy," "I'm taking care of the kids alone"), I felt like I was drowning again, grasping for a life rope they were never going to throw me. With only a few sentences, I could step over an invisible line, becoming a stereotype: the bitter, discarded wife ranting about her villainous husband.

I told myself to be graceful, easy. I told myself not to say too much. I put on my summer dresses. I went to cocktail parties. I did "tide rides" in Vineyard Sound and group walks in Chilmark. I bought hostess gifts. I smiled at my dinner partners. I made small talk on the pier, about the weather, about the kids, as I stood there, in my bathing suit, alone among the married couples, wanting to die.

———

James returned to the Vineyard in July. I knew he was coming. I had begged him to rent a house so the girls could see him, but I was still shocked when a friend texted me that he had been spotted in his tennis whites, circling the courts, looking for a game. She said that some people turned away as he approached. Others acted like everything was normal, and stood with him, chatting. One couple invited him over for a drink. When someone told him they were sorry to hear about our split, he replied, "Life is funny sometimes."

I had suggested he rent a house near the club, so the girls could bike to him with ease. It would be fun for them to be closer to their friends. I sent him multiple listings. But he said the houses were too expensive. He chose a rental deep in the woods of a neighboring development, half of a house still occupied by the owners. He did not bring his jeep or rent a car, instead using Finn's electric bike to get around. He planned to come on weekends, arriving Friday evening and leaving Sunday afternoon.

The rental had three bedrooms, but he told me he couldn't have the girls there for meals or overnights. I offered to leave our house on Friday evenings so they could have dinner at home. I timed my absence carefully, leaving just before he arrived, returning just after he promised to depart, by 8 p.m.

The first time, when I returned at 8:15 p.m., I found him on our deck. It was a beautiful night, the sun was nearly at the horizon, casting a golden glow over the water and our lawn, the magic hour when we used to watch the kids play soccer. James put his left hand on the chair next to him. His ring finger was bare. He said, cheerfully, "Flo! Come watch the sunset with me."

It felt like an arrow, him using that tender name, the name of my childhood, the name Lynn had used in our most wrenching conversations. James had called me "Flo" through-out our marriage, but it felt awful now to hear it on his lips, like he still had access to that part of me. The casualness, like the exclamation mark on my birthday, felt intolerable.

I stood on the deck, several feet from him. I did not sit down. He grinned, looking at the lake, at the descending sun, not at me. He asked, "Other than that other thing, are you having a great time here?"

I said, "You cannot call me that anymore."

I walked to my bedroom, closed the door, and waited for him to leave. I thought, *I should have padlocked the gate.*

He came up two more weekends but abandoned the rental by early August. He said, "I don't like how I feel here."

————

Taylor Swift's album *folklore* was released on July 24, Su-san's birthday. I had never been an avid fan, but it felt like the album was written especially for me. There were songs about illicit affairs, the end of a relationship ("you never gave a warning sign"), heartbreak, mad women. It became the soundtrack of my summer. I abandoned books and podcasts. I pressed play, again and again.

Susan came to visit us for her birthday, as she did every year. We always greeted her with a themed party—Western, Hawaiian, basketball, dogs—decorating the table with props, wearing costumes. The theme always related to something that had happened that year, a trip or new interest. In 2020, I picked a beach theme, in part because of our love of sea glass and the ocean. But it was really because Susan had given me

another helpful metaphor, one she reminded me of in almost
every call. I was in the surf, and giant waves, delivered by
James or someone else, kept hitting me. I had to let them
take me down, find my footing again, and stand up before
the next one arrived.

Finn did not come with Susan. He was stubborn in his
desire to stay in Sagaponack with his friends and my cousin.
It was as if coming to the Vineyard, touching down on the
island, would thrust him into the reality of the divorce. He
didn't say any of this, but I felt it—his fear, his avoidance.

On the night of Susan's birthday, Evie made linguini with
clams we had gathered from the lake. She stuffed the grape
leaves we found on the edge of the lawn and grilled them.
She made a yogurt dipping sauce with freshly chopped parsley, dill, and mint from our garden. She said, "See, Mom, I
can do this for us."

I felt my heart drop when she said it, this beautiful girl,
only fifteen, trying to fill in the space her father had left, trying to make it easier for me. But I was relieved too, grateful
that she was giving us the things we worried would be lost
forever—the specific tastes of summer, of our life as a family, the love James had provided through food.

Susan overlapped with James for one day, on one of his
weekend visits. He came over to the house to set up his boat.
Susan stayed in the guest room, the room with Fortnite, and
watched him as he crossed the lawn in bare feet, carrying
life jackets. She said seeing him filled her with a desperate
sadness. In that moment, he did not look elated. He seemed
older, slower. Like he was lost.

———

In August, the juvenile ospreys started to fish. They flew over the lake and plunged into the water, emerging vertically, often coming up with nothing, but occasionally with fish in their talons. Like their parents, they always carried the fish with the head facing forward.

They started flying higher in the sky, farther over the lake, sometimes disappearing into the expanse of Vineyard Sound, perhaps exploring other lakes on the island, or the waters of Cape Cod, returning to their nest after each journey. They swooped low too, through the trees, over the pool, whistling, convening with us as we swam. We looked up, waved, and yelled, "Hi, Ossey!" as James had taught us to do.

———

In the heat of early August, when the club was the most crowded, I encouraged the girls to have friends over. I bought bagels, Totino's pizza rolls, Double Stuf Oreos, Doritos. I filled the fridge with juice pouches, sodas, chocolate milk. I baked cookies and cakes and placed them in stands on the kitchen island. I put jars of gummy bears and malted milk balls on the counter of the bar near the front door.

They came in droves, sometimes as many as twenty of them, boys and girls, a range of ages, Carrie's group of middle schoolers, Evie's group of teenagers. They sat in the kitchen, eating, toasting things, watching TV. They swam in the pool and lounged on floats—unicorns, swans, and flamingos. There was loud music and peals of laughter. They used our electric bikes to go back and forth to the club, two on each seat, their long hair flying behind them. Girls slept over almost every night, filling every available bed, every bunk. I locked up the wine and liquor, and I had to shut down what seemed like a real party developing in the garage one night, but generally, I didn't scold or direct them. They liked that I wanted them there, that our house wasn't ruled by a stern, unified, married couple. I washed their dishes, ordered new pool floats when they popped, placed their flip-flops and Birkenstocks by the front door so they could find them. They sat with me in the living room, chatting, our bare feet on the coffee table.

I didn't do any of this when James was there, and I wouldn't have done it if he hadn't left. I was always wary of a crowd, of things getting out of control, of messes. I had been brittle. But in my new state, I loved it. It made me feel good, all that happiness and noise and chaos. Something in me had loosened. I thought, *This is something I can do as a single person. This is a silver lining.*

———

At the end of August, there was a chill in the early-morning air. The sun set earlier each night, disappearing well before 8 p.m. We started wearing sweaters at night, jeans instead of dresses. The mood of the osprey family seemed to shift, as did ours. We knew we had to return to Manhattan, our other island, soon. The ospreys were also readying themselves to migrate south, flying at great heights, farther and farther away, like they were taking test runs for their long journey, one that would test their mettle.

———

We drove back to New York on Labor Day. I packed the Toyota with our suitcases, with the sweaters and boots, the textbooks and cellos we'd brought up in March. I felt anxious about having to face real life, a life without my husband, but I was also eager to go, to turn the next page, to move us all forward.

When we entered the apartment, I could tell James was gone. The air was different. I walked to his closet and opened the doors. It was empty except for one of my father's pinstriped suits (my father's custom suits fit James perfectly) and a light blue linen shirt belonging to Susan's late boyfriend. The sight of them felt like another rejection, of both men who had been important to me. Of men James used to admire.

James's desk was completely empty except for the kids' passports, still placed neatly in the corner. He had always been responsible for their passports, for our travel. Seeing the tidy stack felt like a punch: *This will not be his job anymore.*

In the bathroom, his combs and gum were gone. The medicine cabinet was empty.

I walked around the living room, the kitchen, the TV area. It looked intact. There was no sign of anything missing. As I stood there, scanning the living room, I realized that everything else in the apartment had come from me—the furniture, the art, the books, the objects. There was no trace of him having ever been there or of his having left, even though we had lived there, together, for seventeen years. He had taken his things—his suits, his gold coins, his

documents, Mark's posthumous novel from the bookshelf—
but those were small things, things that were unremarkable
in their absence. I thought, *Was he ever really here?*

———

My first night back in New York, I met my Swedish friend,
Maria, at an Italian restaurant on Spring Street. It was open
only for outdoor seating, at tables widely spaced on the un-
even sidewalk. It was still hot and humid, nearly eighty degrees at 6 p.m.

Maria had texted with me during the bleakest hours of
the spring and summer, the endless dark nights, never failing to answer. She and I had met in 2006 at our children's
school; her middle daughter was in Finn's class, her youngest
in Evie's. We grew close when she lost a friend to cancer a
year after Lynn died. As I approached the restaurant, I saw
her sitting at a small table. I felt emotional seeing her for the
first time since February.

We still had to wear masks, pulling them down to talk,
back up when the waitress approached to take our orders.
We ordered the restaurant's house cocktail, something with
tequila and lime served over a giant ice cube.

Maria and I never engaged in small talk. We always spoke
honestly, immediately. As we sat with our drinks, I started
to cry. I didn't weep with abandon anymore, but tears appeared slowly, quietly, streaming down my face, often without me realizing it.

I said, "I still don't understand. I thought he loved me."

She said, "I know. He did. I saw it. Every time he came in
a room. Every time you looked at each other." It was a relief

to hear her say it. A confirmation. James leaving didn't make sense to her either.

We sat in silence for a few minutes.

She asked, "How does it feel to be in the apartment?"

I answered, "Awful. I don't know how to do this. I don't know how to stop missing him."

She said, "It will take time."

Our appetizers arrived. She placed a spoonful of salad, a slice of mozzarella, on my plate.

I said, "I'm so scared." I wasn't sure what I was referring to—being alone, taking care of the kids without James, COVID, what would happen in the divorce. It was all of it.

She took a sip of her drink. She said, "I don't think you have to be afraid of the divorce. He will be fair to you."

I said, "I'm not sure."

She said, "You were partners for twenty years. He will make sure you're okay."

I exhaled, believing for a moment, that it would be easy, that it would be fair. Even with the prenup. He would be kind.

———

In September, the kids returned to school, mostly on Zoom. Evie was a sophomore at a boarding school in Delaware, but they were not allowed to return to campus until mid-October. Carrie and Finn's school was hybrid, alternating each day between in-person and online. Carrie was in seventh grade, still wearing a uniform—pleated skirts, white polo shirts, cardigan sweaters. Finn was a senior and applying to college, a process I knew I would have to manage alone.

I mapped a new walk equal in length to my loop in the Vineyard, west to the river, south to the Battery, north to 14th Street, and, finally, down Broadway, the spine of lower Manhattan. I made dinner for the kids. I walked the dog early in the morning and late at night. The days went by very slowly.

Two weeks after our return, I received an envelope in the mail. It was slim and white, certified with a green post office form affixed to the back, mixed in with the catalogs and bills. I opened it in the kitchen in the early evening, leaning against the island. It contained two pages, stapled together. On the first page, there was a legal caption. I was being summoned. James was asking the court to grant him a divorce. He was asking the court to enforce our prenup.

I knew he wanted a divorce, but I was still stunned by the speed of it, by the words, by the request to enforce the prenup. He had offered me the house and the apartment in the first days after his exit, but the filing meant that he would now claim his share of both properties.

His attorney's name was listed. I didn't recognize it; it was a man, not the female lawyer who had found the prenup in document storage.

I called James on his cell phone. I knew it wouldn't be a good conversation. I knew he would give me nothing. But I couldn't stop myself from calling. He answered on the second ring, like he was waiting for the call.

I said, "Why are you doing this to me?"

He replied, "I'm not doing anything to you."

I said, "You left us. You've never told me why."

His voice was calm, cold. "I didn't leave you. I changed residences."

I felt myself spin, losing control. "You DID leave. You told me you were leaving me! You told me you were continuing your affair! You left me alone to take care of the girls. To deal with COVID by myself." I sobbed through my words, as I did when he first left, when I begged for some explanation.

He said, in a singsong voice, like a taunting child, "Boo-hoo. Poor Belle. Always the victim."

He had never spoken to me like this before; he had never mocked me.

Then, loud and pointed, "You were in a nice house on Martha's Vineyard. You had everything you needed. I paid my share of the bills. What was so hard about that?"

He was right. I had everything I needed, I was more privileged than ninety-nine percent of the world. The same set of facts had been recast in his hands, molded, again, into a different narrative. In his version, I was lucky. In his version, he hadn't done anything wrong. In his version, he had never left.

Was he right? Had I made it all up? Had I spun a story that was false, that unfairly made me the victim and him the villain?

———

In late September, I drove back to the Vineyard to collect our forgotten belongings and to close down the house. Susan stayed with the girls at the apartment. As soon as I arrived, I went to look for the ospreys. The nest was empty. I looked up at the sky, hoping to see one of them flying above me. I listened for their familiar squawk. I saw birds overhead, a similar silhouette, but they were crows, dark and menacing.

I sat down in James's chair, the one he used to watch the sunset, and waited. But they did not appear. They were gone.

In the still-warm September air, I felt the chill of what I'd lost—James, my marriage, my intact family, my understanding of who my husband had been, the layers of protection built up over twenty years, all the things that had made me feel safe, all the things that had placed me in the world. It was just me now—my bones and my brain, the cells of my skin, my breath, in and out. As I sat there, I could feel all of it, all of me.

I tried to reassure myself. *The ospreys will come back. I will be here to see it.*

Part IV

Once they leave their summer home, ospreys use air currents to speed their flight down the coast, soaring over highways, lakes, and rivers. They cover hundreds of miles each day, thousands by the time they reach their final destination. The trip can be as short as a week or as long as a month.

During their journey, ospreys may encounter predators, storms, or hurricanes. These obstacles can blow them off course, slowing their progress, forcing them to take cover for several days. In some cases, the event is fatal.

———

As the kids settled into school, I decided to make the apartment more reflective of me, even though I wasn't yet sure who that was. I knew I wanted to shed the spare aesthetic James and I had adopted together. I wanted the space to feel more feminine, warmer. I gave away his white desk and bought a new one in a warm, burled wood. I framed photographs of Lynn, my father, my grandparents. I hung watercolors of flowers Susan found in her basement. I ordered a bright green wallpaper with cranes and dragonflies for the small bathroom near the kitchen. I hung pale pink pendulum lights over our dinner table. James hated wallpaper, pendulum lights, and anything colorful.

While I added color to the apartment, I removed it from my wardrobe. Charmaine, my brother's wife, helped me go through my closet. She is the most stylish person I know, and the most fun. She was determined to get me to a better place, to make it all a bit less grim. I had hung the kids' puffy winter parkas in the space where James's suits had been. Charmaine took them all out, carried them out of the room, and crammed them into the hall closet.

She said, "No kid clothes in here. This is Flo World now."

We laughed, but it was a happy thought. All that space. A room of my own.

She said, "Now we're going to turn you into a chic French divorcée."

I laughed again. "Yes!" It was an image that appealed to me, rather than the matronly, discarded wife I'd been holding in my head.

I did not inherit my grandmother's and mother's innate style, their famous glamour. My family's entries on the International Best Dressed List ended with me. I avoided the world in which fashion mattered, the women who dressed for society photographers. I was too shy for it. Until my thirties, I didn't care about clothes at all. But in my new state, I could see how clothing could help me forge an identity, one that I liked.

Charmaine and I made a pile of clothes to sell. We got rid of anything floral, anything patterned, anything dowdy. And everything that was now too big. She organized my closets, including those taken over from James, in neat rows, the clothes mostly black, navy, gray, white, cream. We tried different outfits and she took photos. She encouraged me to wear shorter skirts and higher heels (but not together). It felt like a huge gift, her helping me to redefine myself, at least on the outside.

But I had almost nowhere to go. With COVID rates still high, there were very few invitations, very few gatherings. I saw my friends now and then, for increasingly cold dinners outside, or for a walk on the Hudson River, and the kids were with me—appearing at dinner, making smoothies in the kitchen, taking showers in my bathroom. But they always ended up in their rooms, their doors closed. I no longer had the noise and chaos of a dozen teenagers coming and going. It was so quiet.

A deep loneliness set in, reminiscent of how I felt in my childhood home. I told myself a story about being alone: the rest of the world, including James, was coupled; James had proven that I was unlovable by leaving me; I would always be alone. This story wrapped around me, through me, like a snake.

———

In late October, I was invited to a dinner party at a town house uptown. I was happy to be included, to have something to do. I wore jeans, a thick navy sweater, new black ballerina flats. We sat at a table in the garden under heat lamps. It was chilly but not yet freezing. I was seated next to the handsome and charismatic host, whom I liked but didn't know well. He was part of James's tennis group.

As we settled into the meal, picking up our knives and forks, he said, "Boy, am I glad you're getting divorced. I'm finally beating James at tennis." He chuckled. "During our match last week, he took a call from you and came back so rattled, he lost. So thank you!"

James and I had not spoken on the phone since the night I had received the summons, and definitely not while he was playing tennis. I didn't know how to answer. *Was I meant to laugh?* I smiled as warmly as I could and tried to reassure myself, *He's trying to break the ice. It's okay.*

Then he said, "I gave James the name of my divorce lawyer." It was the name on the summons. He said, "He represents all the Goldman Sachs guys. He's really tough. He's going to keep you in court for *years*." This man delivered these sentences lightly, like it wasn't a big deal.

Is he trying to help me, telling me this so I can protect myself? Or is it a threat, delivered on behalf of James, to settle quickly or spend the next years of my life in litigation, getting crushed? Or is he just sharing facts that I should take in stride, like a man?

I tried to look busy eating my food while my cheeks burned red in the candlelight. A full-bodied fear rushed through me, a flood of awareness that, while I was navigating my days—walking the dog, making breakfast, checking homework—a deck was being stacked against me.

———

I made appointments with my dentist and my doctors. It felt like I had weathered a storm and I needed to be checked, healed, fixed.

My gynecologist was in Carnegie Hill. I'd started going to her two years before, when my obstetrician had retired. In her exam room, I took off my clothes, put on a hospital gown, stood on the scale, and sat on the table, the paper crinkling under me. The doctor walked in and we had the routine conversation about my health (fine), whether I was in menopause (not yet). I told her about James leaving. I told her I'd been under a lot of stress. She said she was sorry to hear it. She didn't comment on my weight loss.

She examined my breasts and abdomen. I put my legs in the stirrups.

She put on her gloves and said, "You don't work, right?" She put one hand inside me, the other on my stomach, pressing.

I winced from her probing. I said, "No, I'm a lawyer, I do pro bono cases, but nothing full-time. Nothing paid."

She said, "You know, women become less interesting to men when they don't work. It really has a negative impact on marriages. I've seen it a lot."

She pulled her hand out from inside my body, removed her gloves, and tossed them in the garbage. She said my exam was normal and that I could call her for the Pap smear results in a few days. She left the room.

I got dressed as quickly as I could. My legs were shaking so much it was hard to put on my underwear, my jeans.

He left me because I wasn't interesting enough? Because I'd stayed home with the kids?

Maybe this is why he picked the woman with the alliterative name, because she had a serious job?

My gynecologist would not be the only person to imply this over the next year. She was the most explicit, but other people, usually working women, floated the idea. It was an easy answer, one that may have made them feel better, like a guarantee: *If you work, this won't happen to you.*

———

During the fall and winter, our divorce gathered steam. I had engaged a lawyer in the spring, at my family's urging, but she was known as a mediator. Once James had hired the famously aggressive lawyer—the one recommended by his tennis friend—several people told me I was "bringing a knife to a gunfight." So, I hired a new lawyer, a woman, in November. She was smart, elegant, maternal. And tough. I loved her as soon as I met her.

We appeared at hearings in the judge's virtual courtroom— me at my new desk, James in his office in Nolita, looking up at the screen above his desk. We filed our financial statements, tax returns, statements of assets and expenses. All of it—every moment, every appearance, every exchange— hurt me. I took it all personally.

James's demeanor was professional, remote. It felt like we were in a corporate transaction, on opposing sides, a stage with no emotion. But there was something else. I could see it in his eyes as I squinted at my computer screen: a steely, simmering anger.

I had to shift, again, in my understanding of the man I'd been married to. He was not a benign stranger wandering out of my life. He was an adversary, determined to win.

———

That year, we seemed to receive even more Christmas cards than usual, many of them arriving long after the New Year. Day after day they arrived, nearly a hundred images of happy, intact families. It was also the year many couples I knew, my contemporaries, celebrated their twenty-fifth anniversaries, the milestone I would never reach. They posted their wedding photos on Instagram, adding long paragraphs about the success of their marriages, their love for their spouses. Birthday posts seemed to multiply too, odes to terrific husbands, to beautiful wives.

Each card, each post, felt like a dagger. I knew they had nothing to do with me. The senders weren't thinking about me at all. They had great families, good marriages; I understood why they were celebrating. Still, the pain of it was staggering, like the postman was delivering daily bombs, reminders of what I had lost. I was no longer one of them. I was something different now.

When I opened an envelope or looked at a post, I wanted to scream, *I thought I had that too! I loved and was loved in the same way! There is nothing different about us!*

I rarely posted on Instagram, but I had sent out Christmas cards for seventeen years, unaware of how it might feel to receive them. I had been unintentionally smug, flaunting my good fortune.

I didn't send one in 2020. I would never send one again.

When each card arrived, I tore it in half, ripping through children and babies, husbands and wives, through smiling faces, and dropped it in the trash. I unfollowed people. I quit Instagram, rejoined, and quit again.

———

I dreaded Christmas. We'd done the same thing for fourteen years, since before Carrie was born: we flew up to Martha's Vineyard early on Christmas morning; we wore matching Christmas pajamas and the dog wore a Santa suit; James cooked breakfast—scrambled eggs, bacon, sausages; we opened presents I'd mailed up; we went bowling; we took family walks, forcing the kids out of the house, down the paths in the woods; we watched movies; James organized a skating party at the local rink, dividing the ice between hockey players and ice skaters, inviting anyone we knew on the island, using the Rangers helmets and gloves he'd collected, serving chocolate chip cookies and thermoses of hot chocolate; James cooked elaborate dinners, including, always, Swedish meatballs; we opened our best wine. It was the same, year after year. We loved it.

Doing it without James, with his seat empty, felt impossible. Thanksgiving that year, at Susan's house in Sagaponack, was strange and chaotic—twenty people, including my brother's family and my cousins, all of us cooking in masks. The kids did not feel James's absence the way they would on Christmas.

James had texted, "You should take them to the Vineyard." I couldn't tell, in text, whether he felt sad about missing it, about handing the holiday over to me.

I debated doing something different, going somewhere new, but it wasn't possible. COVID was still raging. The first variant had arrived in the United States in November.

I thought about Evie making linguini and clams and grape

leaves in July, her wisdom in preserving what was important to our family. I made a decision: *We will go to the Vineyard. I will do everything the same way. I will fill in the hole.*

To make it easier, and more cheerful, I asked Susan to come. She agreed, understanding the mission. She cooked the sausages while I whisked the eggs. She built fires while I rolled Swedish meatballs. We watched movies. We went for family walks. The bowling alley and skating rink were closed, but everything else was the same.

There was a palpable sadness in every activity, but I also felt a determination, in each of us, to make it okay for one another. It reminded me of returning to my family's house in Water Mill after my father's death—Susan, my brother, and I wept in his closet, clutching his clothes and his pipes, stunned by his absence. But we tried to carry on, to help one another through it. This was not the same—James was alive and well in New York, perhaps spending the holiday with another woman. But the shock of his absence, the grief of moving forward without a member of the family, without our leading man, felt familiar.

On Christmas Day, after we'd eaten breakfast and opened presents, Susan and I sat facing each other in the upholstered chairs in the living room, our feet on the coffee table. The girls were on the floor next to us, playing with a new American Girl camper (even as teenagers, they loved American Girl). Finn was lying on the couch on the other side of the room, trying to solve the Rubik's Cube I'd put in his stocking. The fire roared. Classical music filled the room. It wasn't perfect, but it was nice.

Susan mouthed to me, "What the fuck?"

I knew what she meant. *What was so bad about this? Why would he give it up?*

———

In January 2021, James and I exchanged our "production," the documents required in discovery. His statements arrived all at once, in a zip file from my lawyer's paralegal. As I read through it, clicking on document after document, statement after statement, my skin started to burn, like my nerve endings were on fire. I saw year after year of his earnings, investment returns and bonuses, accumulating into a fortune, which he held in his name alone.

I knew he'd been doing well, but I didn't know the numbers, I hadn't read the tax returns he'd placed in front of me to sign. I'd assumed we were both stretching ourselves to afford our life together. I didn't know that he'd earned millions of dollars each year. I didn't know how his earnings had added up. He had known everything about me, where every dollar of mine sat, but I had known nothing about him. He had not hidden it. I had chosen not to look. I had chosen not to know.

I found the printed agenda from our meeting with our lawyer in July 2019. I remembered what she had said about Susan ending tuition payments. I saw the last bullet about the prenup. The thing we hadn't done. The thing I had agreed to wait on.

Now James could claim his ownership stake in both properties. He could walk away with his assets. He could become a partner at a hedge fund, where his wealth would increase exponentially, unencumbered by me.

Was this the explanation? Was there a clock ticking, one I hadn't heard? A countdown to get out? A tipping point?

Or was the timing only a coincidence, career success meeting marital fatigue at one precise point, like lines on a graph—an explosive intersection neither of us could have predicted?

———

That winter, I stopped sleeping. Or, really, I slept in bursts of only an hour or so, waking up repeatedly, at 1 a.m., 2 a.m., 4 a.m., in a heart-racing panic. I switched sides of the bed each night, from my side to James's, on the mattress he had bought and abandoned, trying to fill the empty space, but it didn't help. I slept with my laptop in my bed, turning it on each time I woke, restarting a familiar show, *Schitt's Creek* or *Friends,* something to lull me, to force me to stop thinking. It worked for a bit, I would fall asleep again, but only briefly. At 5 a.m., I'd give up, even though it was still dark out. I'd turn on the lights, make my coffee, feed the dog. I was always relieved the night was over.

What I felt at night, when I woke up every hour, was ice-cold fear. My lawyer was preparing a counterclaim to James's filing. It was a direct challenge to James, to how he wanted the divorce to play out.

I had little chance of success. But my lawyer and I agreed that I needed to try. The document took shape, slowly, painfully. When I lay in bed during the bleak hours, sentences floated through my mind. I knew every word. I knew every number. I knew my side of our story.

———

As January progressed, another narrative started forming in my consciousness, sentences and phrases, details of textbooks and cellos, gnocchi and whiskey sours, the cold tile of the bathroom floor. It was the story of James leaving, the emotional layers, the aspects of our parting that a legal document could not tell. I felt an all-consuming itch to put it down on paper, to record it. In the dark of one morning, I sat down at my desk and started writing. It was the first time I'd written anything (other than legal briefs) in thirty-five years. Since Greg told me I couldn't write.

It felt primal, wanting to get it on the page. James had twisted the story of our ending into something that made him comfortable, one in which he hadn't even left me. The dinner party hosts, the women on porches, the chorus of opining voices had also tried to turn it into something else. And so had I, at times, believing what James and the others said. Writing it felt like a flashlight in that haze. *This is what happened.*

But it was more than just journaling or venting. I was deliberate in the art of it. Other than crafts with the kids and some elaborate baking, I hadn't done anything creative in my life as an adult, as a mother. I liked that part of the writing, developing my skill, finding exactly the right word, establishing a rhythm. And I liked that it was just for me, with no other purpose.

I remember trying to write once while I was married, sitting down at my desk, attempting to capture something about my father, about his death. Nothing came. I could barely get a sentence on the page. I couldn't find a thread, a road in. I felt locked. But the ten months on my own, the winter of sleepless nights, the practice writing the counterclaim—it all seemed to have given me a key.

Looking back on those early days of writing, when I think of myself sitting at my desk, I see a woman stripped of the soft layers built up over twenty years of marriage—her trust in her husband, the comfort of their life together, the way their marriage placed her in the world. Without the layers, the padding, the woman at the desk can feel things, can see things. She has a way in.

Within a couple of weeks, I had a rough draft. At almost the exact moment I finished it, a friend emailed me the link to a memoir-writing class. She was signing up for it and thought I might like to join her. She remembered that I used to love to write. I thought, *This is a sign. I need to do this.* I could still hear the voice in my head, so familiar after three decades, telling me I was not a writer. I decided I had to do it anyway.

The class, on Zoom, was gentle and supportive. People read their work and we clapped. The teacher did not allow any critique. There was no danger of a Greg. But I didn't read anything. I didn't say anything. I evaded the teacher's challenge to write for at least thirty minutes a day. But I did the in-class writing exercises. I listened to the writers who came to talk to us about writing their memoirs. And I kept looking at my piece about James leaving. I added more detail. I cut unnecessary words. I fiddled with sentences. It felt good to return to the pages each time, pulling them up on the screen, like old friends, places to rest my head.

———

In February, James moved from the Beekman apartment into his new apartment on Park Row. He turned his second bedroom into a home office, even though he had a large office three subway stops away. There was no bedroom for the kids. He kept in touch with them by text, always kindly, and took them out to an occasional dinner, but he continued to refuse a daily role in their lives.

My lawyer sent James a 50/50 custody agreement, the arrangement I would have wanted as a child. I thought we would reach resolution quickly, given that it was an equal split. I thought, by then, James would have realized his mistake, that he would want to claim his time with the kids. What followed stunned me more than any custody dispute ever could: James returned the document stripped of all his time, including vacations, holidays, weeks during the summer. He included only dinner on Thursday nights.

He said he didn't want to make the kids go back and forth between us. He said he didn't want to force them to rotate holidays. He said they were too old—now thirteen, sixteen, and eighteen—to have to do any of this, that they were "fully formed human beings." He said they could decide when they wanted to see him. He said they could call him when they needed him. I think he believed, genuinely, that he was making a selfless choice, that he was making things easier for them. I tried to convince him of what would be gained by living with them, the access you get when you make them breakfast, when they ask for help with homework, when they come home from a sleepover or a night out, when you take them on a trip. But he was resolute. He would not do it.

Several of James's male friends echoed his rationale to me, nearly verbatim: *Aren't your kids too old to go back and forth? Won't he be available to them if they need him?* I was startled each time I heard this, his exact words and phrasing, their support for his decision.

What would they have said about me, had I given up all my time with my kids, had I decided not to have a room for a child as young as twelve?

A few women excused it, chalking it up to men being "hapless," "incapable."

Is this a valid excuse? My father was not a natural at parenting, yet he claimed us, he made a home for us, he tried.

For almost a year, I tried to engage James in parenting, especially when I needed help. I told him how worried I was about Carrie, bearing the greatest toll of our separation as the youngest, her tears late at night. I sent him detailed updates from Evie's school, their stringent COVID rules, calling him when I had to pick her up in Delaware at 1 a.m. after she had a positive test. I forwarded him alerts when Finn missed a class. I still wanted a partner in all of it. Sometimes he showed up. When Finn had surgery, he was very present, helping me manage Finn's pain, speaking to the doctor, picking up his medications.

But more often, for everyday issues, he responded with irritation. Or he seemed mystified, like he had no idea what to do, like the kids were people he'd only recently met. Eventually, I stopped asking for help. It was too painful to be turned down, to encounter someone who felt like a distant relative when I expected to find my children's father.

I could have demanded, more forcefully, that he host them for overnights, that he make a bedroom for them, or at least for Carrie. I could have gotten angry when the Thursday night dinners stopped. As the pandemic receded, I could have insisted that he take them away on vacations. I could have planned trips for him.

I didn't do any of these things.

It felt dangerous, forcing it, when he didn't choose it. It felt like opening the door to more hurt, more rejection, for the kids. I encouraged them to call him, to text him back, to go to dinner when he proposed it. I shared good news—their grades, Carrie's high-school acceptances, Finn and Evie's college acceptances. But otherwise, I let go of the rope. It was burning my hands, pulling so forcefully in the opposite direction.

Continuing to reach out also pulled against a boundary I was trying to draw, minimizing my contact with James, avoiding conflict, especially as he sued me in matrimonial court. I told the doormen in my building to call me when he wanted to come upstairs to drop off mail (he would sail past them, like the owner he was). I created a forwarding system that pushed his emails to a special folder, so I could choose when to open them. Sometimes, when his texts were too harsh, I blocked his number. I was creating safe spaces for myself. I was padlocking my gates.

But still, I doubted myself: *Was I being vindictive by not trying harder? Should the parent who remains always take this on, no matter what they encounter in their former partner? Should I have kept all my doors open? Is this how to be a good mother? Is this how to be graceful?*

———

Over President's Day weekend, Carrie and I visited Susan at her house in Sagaponack. We celebrated Valentine's Day on Saturday, decorating the breakfast table with chocolate hearts and roses. Susan gave us pink sweaters; we gave her red socks. It was freezing and windy, too cold to walk. Carrie and I watched a romantic comedy, *Valentine's Day,* in bed. I pretended to pay attention, but I was really doing the *Times* crossword puzzle on my phone. Any movie with a love story, a wedding, a tale of destiny between two people, had become too hard to watch.

Saturday crosswords were ridiculously hard, sometimes taking me days to complete, but they were getting a little easier, the payoff of doing the puzzles every day, learning the clues they repeated, the style of answer they were looking for. My brother and I competed for speed, sending each other screenshots of our best times. He always beat me by a large margin, sometimes finishing the Saturday puzzle in under ten minutes.

Susan came into the room, holding the draft of the counterclaim I'd given her to read. She motioned for me to join her in the hallway. Once out of earshot of Carrie, she said, "Flo, I don't know if you should do this." She looked scared. Her face was pale, her left hand, holding the papers, was shaking.

"Why not?"

She said, "He's going to be angry." I had never seen her look so worried. She had tried to protect me since I was three years old, guarding me with her thighs as I hid behind her. She was still trying to shield me now, four decades later. If I filed the counterclaim, she might not be able to save me. I would be standing out there on my own.

I looked at the pages in her hand. "I know. He doesn't expect me to fight back."

She said, "I'm scared he will punish you for it."

I took the pages from her and sighed. "It feels awful, all of it, filing it or not filing it, both options feel awful."

Carrie and I returned home on Monday, three days before the filing deadline. I read the counterclaim closely again. I went back and forth, trying to decide. I nearly vibrated with fear.

It would be easier, safer, to let the divorce proceed as James wanted it to. To trust that he would be fair to me in the end. That's what everyone, including James, expected me to do. That was the choice that would keep me safe.

But why should I trust James to be fair to me? Why would it serve me, or my children, to be silent?

There was something growing in me, an almost nihilistic desire to set flame to the remaining structures of my former life, to the very safety I clung to, to the fiction that I could depend on anyone other than myself for protection, to the idea that being quiet was the only way to be good. And a deepening of an instinct, within me since the first days after James left, that the truth was the only possible foundation for what would come next.

On Thursday, February 18, I wrote to my lawyer, "I'm ready. Let's file it."

———

In early 2021, the pandemic continued to keep New Yorkers home. We were still masked, still avoiding gatherings, still scared. Even so, as a newly single woman, everywhere I turned, I seemed to encounter pressure to date, an expectation that I enter the market. When I ran into a friend or acquaintance who knew my story, they often asked the same questions, in succession:

"Is he still with that woman?"

It was always a jolt to be asked about her. I had disciplined my brain not to think about the affair, about her face, her name, but here she was again, delivered to my consciousness.

I answered, "I don't know." I didn't.

And then, "Are you dating?"

When they asked this, I felt a deep discomfort, a sense of being misunderstood. And a trace of anger.

"No."

My closest people did it too. They encouraged me to join dating apps, to spread the word that I wanted to be fixed up. It was as though time were running out. There were so few available men, and I was nearly fifty-two. I'd better find one fast.

It all came from a good place. My friends wanted me to be happy again, to be healed, to have fun. They had faith that I could, and would, find someone. I had several divorced friends who had met wonderful partners after a period of conscientious dating. I still believed in love and relationships. And I *was* lonely. I continued to feel the ache, in my apartment alone, night after night. I continued to feel like an alien at group gatherings, with almost all my friends married or partnered.

Still, I couldn't do it, I couldn't market myself. It wasn't like men were beating down my door, but I couldn't bring myself to indicate, even gently, that I was open to it. I know

I was scared. I could not imagine how I could trust someone again. It wasn't just trusting that they would be faithful,
it was trusting that I could believe in what they presented
to me, that they weren't harboring an alternate self, one I
couldn't see.

Harder to admit was that I was still, in some way, in love
with James, with the version of him that had disappeared.
Since we hadn't unwound from each other while we were
together, my heart and my body were still tied to him, my
husband, the man who continued to appear in my dreams
almost every night. People assumed that once James left, the
moment he walked out the door, my love for him would
vanish too. *But how does one turn that off after twenty-two years?*
How long does it take your unconscious mind to catch up?

I was also anxious about my kids, almost as if they were
babies again and I couldn't risk taking my eyes off them. I
wanted to be as steady for them as possible, as their father
floated away. I remembered my mother's boyfriends, the
way they pulled her from us, how disorienting that felt, to
have a stranger in the house, appearing at breakfast. I would
do it differently. I had heard the term "potted plant years"—
teenagers may not want to talk to you, but they like you to
be around, to be there when they go out, to be there when
they return. I wanted to be a potted plant for my children.

But the trace of anger I felt when I was asked about dating, or encouraged to work at it, was because of the subtext: *You won't be okay until you have another man to protect*
you. We won't be comfortable with you, with the state of things,
until you are back in the norm. If you don't recouple, we will place

*you in the dreaded category of divorced women—those who haven't
"moved on."*

Why? Why did I have to secure a man to be okay?

Even in my loneliness, even with the script I read myself
about being unlovable, I rejected this storyline.

*That is not my happy ending. That is not my definition of mov-
ing on. That is not my definition of success.*

So, except for a few dinners with an old friend, I did not
date at all.

———

In March, I received my client's green card in the mail. My
law partner and I drove out to Queens to deliver it to her and
her mother. We stood outside on the sidewalk, the four of us
masked, all of us in parkas. We took photos. We hugged. We
felt palpable joy. Our client was now a permanent resident.
She could access federal grants and loans for college. In five
years, she would become a US citizen.

Fueled by the success, we took on a new case. Our new
client, an eight-year-old girl, came to the United States
with her parents for two urgent reasons: her father had been
beaten and jailed for pro-democracy political activities, and
her mother had a serious illness. Her mother could not access
treatment in her home country.

Our client's father promptly filed an asylum application
with the United States Citizenship and Immigration Services
(USCIS), listing his wife and daughter as co-applicants. He
was a teacher but the only work he could find was driving a
taxi in Brooklyn. In March 2020, the same month my fam-

ily and I arrived at our second home, he drove sick people
back and forth to the hospital in his taxi. He soon contracted
COVID and, after being refused an ambulance twice, he
died. He had waited five years for an asylum interview; the
interview notice arrived six months after his death. When
our client and her mother appeared for the interview, they
were told that his death extinguished the asylum claim and
they would have to start again, filing for themselves.

My partner and I sought Special Immigrant Juvenile status for our client in family court and prepared an asylum
application for our client's mother. We drafted affidavits,
memoranda of law, supporting documents. I was better at
it at this point. I didn't cry. I made fewer mistakes. We appeared in family court virtually and our client's application
was approved. She would have to wait years for a green card
(availability is determined by the applicant's country of ori-
gin), but this was a critical first step.

Our client's mother faced a greater challenge. Her own
asylum application would almost certainly be denied; the
nexus between her and the political persecution suffered by
her husband was weak. If her application was denied, under
USCIS's current "first in, first out" system, she could be de-
ported within a couple of months, returning to a dangerous
country where she would have no access to the treatment
that kept her alive. She was faced with a terrible choice: stay
underground and risk losing her health insurance and access
to treatment, or file for asylum and risk deportation, separation from her daughter, and a certain death sentence. She
chose the former.

Once again, the rigor of the work, the detail of it, was

absorbing and grounding. It forced me to think about something other than my divorce. It also forced me to acknowledge how myopic, how grandiose, I'd been about my own story. It wasn't just recognizing my comparative good fortune (which was enormous); it was seeing the scope of life, of challenge, of suffering, of what human beings endure; it was a zooming out.

———

Exactly a year after James left me, at the end of March, I texted him late at night. During these hours, I still felt a raw pain lodged in my chest, making it hard to breathe, impossible to sleep.

I wrote, "You never told me what I did wrong in our marriage, why you stopped loving me. It is such an awful thing, after twenty-one years, not to know."

I had hoped something had changed, that he would give me the answer, the lost frames of the movie, something to help me understand what had happened.

He wrote back, "I wish I could answer your question, something broke in me, it was me and not you, you did nothing wrong."

It should have been a relief, hearing again that it was not my fault. But it felt like a fresh blow—the answer without an answer, the refusal to fill in the blanks, the assumption that one sentence would be enough.

———

I visited Evie at her boarding school in Delaware as often as I could, as often as the school would allow me. They had very strict rules during the pandemic. Parents could not enter buildings. The students could not leave the gates. It was like they were in prison. I brought Evie and her friends Taco Bell, Chick-fil-A, Chipotle. We sat outside on the lawn, in the cold, pulling down our paper masks to eat.

I often stopped to see Anna, my friend from boarding school, at her house in Wilmington. On one visit, as we walked over the hills of a nearby golf course with her five dogs—four dachshunds and a black lab—she said, "You are so different now."

"What do you mean?"

She answered, "You are different than when you were married."

She walked ahead, pulled by one of the dachshunds, the curls of her dark hair bouncing. I felt a defensiveness rise in me. *Do not go there.*

She continued, "I don't know how to describe it. You were much harder to know then."

I replied, with an edge, "You weren't easy either."

She answered, "I know. My mother getting sick broke me open." It was true. She had become more vulnerable, softer, when her mother was diagnosed with lung cancer.

I relaxed a little with her admission. "Okay, what do you mean about me?"

She continued, "You seemed tense, stressed. You had walls up."

We walked for a few minutes in silence.

She said, "I'm sorry. I'm upsetting you."

She *was* upsetting me. Whenever I encountered the implication that I hadn't been a great person when I was married, a great wife, I went on alert, ready to shoot. My narrative was dependent on me being blameless, on James having no valid reason to leave. If I let in the competing idea, my entire story, the one in which I was an angelic victim, would crumble. Even with James's assurance that it hadn't been my fault, my greatest fear was still the simplest explanation: he left because of me. I hadn't made James happy. Worse, I had made him unhappy. It may not have been any more complicated than that.

I can make a list of things James may have grown to dislike about me. I could be tightly wound, stressed and anxious about plans, upset if something small or big went wrong with the kids, when travel went awry. I did not share his interests in tennis, hockey, or ancient archaeology, and I didn't try to learn about them. I nagged him to do things like walk the dog and pick up dinner in Chinatown. I was irritated when he left silverware in a pile in the corner of the sink instead of loading it in the dishwasher. I was not as skinny or desirable as I'd been when we met. I may not have made him feel appreciated enough for how hard he worked, for the ways he provided for our family. I hated his favorite band, Dinosaur Jr., and told him to turn it down, or turn it off, when he played their albums loudly from his laptop.

Two years before he left, when we were on a trip with a group of couples, I struggled with the social dynamic among the women; it felt like a high-school clique I could not break into. I had a meltdown in our hotel room, exacerbated by having sprained my ankle, an injury everyone seemed to find annoying. James was unsympathetic to my plight. He was mad. And cold. As I thought about my failings, that night returned to me—my discomfort, his irritation.

Maybe this was enough to answer the ultimate question, the one he had refused to answer for me? Maybe he was sparing my feelings by not telling me that it was all because of me? Maybe I had to own it?

And maybe I failed to see the signs of his unhappiness—going to bed so early, how rote his routine was (work, tennis, television), the cocktail as soon as he walked through the door. I should have seen it and done something about it. It was my fault for not figuring it out.

Some people say the end of a marriage is always fifty-fifty, that each partner bears equal responsibility. "It takes two to tango." I'd heard this about other divorces, often about the wife who was left, even when the husband had engaged in years of betrayals and lies: *She wasn't fun enough. She was too focused on the kids. She didn't pay enough attention to him.* I'm sure similar things were said about me.

But is it fifty-fifty when the unhappy person doesn't say they are unhappy? When they act like everything is exactly as they want it to be, leaving their partner to guess? When they don't give their partner a warning, a beat to change course, to grow, before betraying them, before cutting the cord?

And couldn't you make your own list? Isn't there always a list?

Anna and I scaled a hill, the dogs running ahead of us. I asked, "How do you think I'm different now?"

She paused. "You are lighter, easier, more relaxed. You laugh more, smile more. There aren't any hidden rules. I don't have to translate your mood. You tell me right away when I make you mad, which honestly delights me. You are speaking your mind."

I smiled. "Okay, go on."

She continued, "When something goes off course, you

let it go. If not right away, then after some time thinking about it, digesting it. You seem to be letting go of a bigger set of cultural standards, of some sort of externally imposed idea of who you should be."

I recognized what she was saying. I *was* more relaxed. I *did* laugh more. I could linger in conversations. I could let things go. I could welcome dozens of rowdy teenagers in my home without flinching. Something in me had opened. Something in me had mellowed.

What was it about losing my marriage that made me looser? Why was I more at ease with myself?

It was everything—the quiet of the pandemic, remaining single, all that time on my own, being with myself. It was having everything I had counted on collapse so suddenly, forcing me to let go of the idea that I could control outcomes. It was the loss of my identity as a wife, my identity as part of a married couple. I had to get comfortable existing outside the norm, outside of what had once been my ideal.

As Anna and I turned back toward her house, I thought, *Maybe it is more than that? Maybe James's distance, his not quite being there, made me closed? Maybe steering the ship of our family on my own, carrying the emotional load alone, was what made me tense?*

Anna continued, "I know you had everything you wanted. I know you loved him, and you loved your marriage, your family. But you are yourself again, more like the Belle I knew in 1985."

I answered, "I think that's true." I paused and thought for the first time, *I like myself more now.*

———

While our divorce was pending, James and I had to continue sharing bills, expenses, taxes. He was still in charge. I had to annotate credit card bills even more precisely, justifying every expense. He had to approve any significant expenditures in advance. He was even more stringent, more insistent that we control spending, that we cut back. His care, his authority, continued, in some way, to make me feel safe. And I was spared, for a time, handling it all myself, having to understand it, having to face the reality of my financial life. I still believed I couldn't do it. I still believed I needed him to protect me.

I also hated it, having to explain myself, having to answer to him, allowing him to make decisions, both big and small. I could no longer convince myself that he was taking care of me. And I could see that the cost for feeling safe was being controlled. They were two sides of the same coin—protection and control.

Some divorced women I knew were still financially entwined with their ex-husbands. The men paid expenses directly. They provided credit cards. They still owned the apartments where their ex-wives lived. It is often a wise and necessary financial choice, to keep these arrangements going. But I knew that once we were divorced, continuing to defer to James, continuing to abandon my own authority, would feel intolerable.

I wrote to my lawyer, "Wherever we end up, I want no overlap in our finances. I want a clean break. I don't want to answer to him ever again."

———

As the weather warmed again, April turning to May, I went out to more dinners with friends, almost always groups of women. I no longer seemed to be a candidate for couples' dinners, a fact I had grown to accept. We were still seated outside at restaurants, on sidewalks, under covered structures, sometimes in claustrophobic cabanas—the bulky architecture of the pandemic.

During these dinners with women I liked, I noticed that they often spoke about their husbands. Sometimes they complained—small things that annoyed them or bigger things, revealing fractures I hadn't known about, unhappiness they had never shared before. It felt generous, an effort to tell me that, while married, their lives were not perfect.

More often, women praised their husbands, sharing a story in passing about how thoughtful they were, how accomplished, how terrific they were as fathers. Or they complimented one another's husbands, trading accolades.

I don't think it was intentional or unkind; it seemed almost unconscious, as if my presence, my story, spurred a reflexive defense in them, of their spouses, their marriages, their families, to reassure not just themselves, but one another, that all was well. I usually agreed with them—their husbands were good men—but still, I felt wounded. They were celebrating the very thing I had lost.

I asked myself, *Maybe it had always happened—these passing comments—and I was only now sensitive to it? Maybe I had done it too, when I'd had a husband?*

And did I really want them to stop? Did I want them to censor themselves because I was at the table? Did I want to be seen as fragile, angry, envious, leading to fewer invitations, fewer intimacies?

After one dinner, I texted a friend in London. She had been divorced for a few years. She had left her husband, but we faced similar challenges. We both parented our children almost alone. We both found ourselves in very married settings while no longer married.

I asked her, "Have you noticed this, the praising of husbands?"

She said, "All the time. It's crazy. I don't think they realize it. When it happens, I completely disassociate; I think about something else, anything else, until the conversation ends."

I started doing the same thing, taking my brain to a different place while I smiled, pretending to listen.

———

Finn graduated from high school in May. Only parents and siblings were allowed to attend the ceremony. Evie was still in boarding school, so it was just me, James, and Carrie. I braced myself for it. We were still awaiting the judge's decision. James had not said anything to me about my counterclaim. I hadn't seen him in months.

I wore a black sleeveless dress and heeled sandals, trying to shield myself in clothes that felt both strong and impersonal. We were all masked, sitting quietly in the church's pews. I looked around for friends, other mothers of graduates. They nodded at me. They knew what I was facing.

James arrived, walking up the aisle in his navy suit, his crisp shirt and tie, his blue mask. I felt the familiar rush of love, the flutter I'd always felt when he appeared. And then the rush of sadness, the chill.

I stood up to let him into the pew, to sit between me and Carrie. As we waited for the ceremony to begin, as he chatted with Carrie, I looked straight ahead, trying to focus my thoughts on Finn. He had finished high school during COVID, during the sudden breakup of our family. And he was going to college. It felt like an epic accomplishment.

During the school year, Finn had continued to resist intimate conversations, about the divorce or anything else, but we'd pushed through each day, each application, each challenge—me as a potted plant, he as a maturing teenager, inching toward the finish line. It was not easy, and we'd done it without James.

I wanted to say to James, *Look what he did! Look what I did!* I wanted my steadiness, my daily effort, my care for our children to be acknowledged. But I had learned that he would not give me that.

When I looked down, I could see James's hand resting on his thigh. My whole body yearned to move closer to him, to press my thigh against his, to thread my fingers through his, as I had so many times before. It was like my body still had not received the message, that this man was no longer mine, that he was someone else.

After the ceremony, families gathered in the schoolyard for a reception. Finn and his friends beamed, their eyes shining, their masks pulled down to smoke cigars, looking like both the boys they had been and the men they were becoming. I took photographs of Finn with James, Finn with Carrie. James took photographs of me with Finn. And then one as a family, Finn and Carrie in the middle, James and I book-ending them.

As we milled around the yard, James seemed breezy, light, unencumbered. There was no sense of tension or danger about what was happening between us, about what was going to happen next.

———

In July, in a short decision delivered by email, the judge dismissed my counterclaim, enforced the prenup, and set a trial date in October. The trial would resolve child support and ownership of our joint property, including the house and the apartment. My lawyer feared that given the enforcement of the prenup, the judge would almost certainly grant James his ownership stake in both homes. She said I would have to hope that James would be kind.

James had not mentioned the counterclaim before the decision, but now he was inflamed by it. He said he would give me only the minimum child support required by law. He said I would have to face the consequences of the prenup, of my failed counterclaim.

In early August, James's lawyer sent a searing letter. He restated the terms of the prenup. He said he assumed I wanted to buy James out of his interests in the house and the apartment, and if so, that we should schedule appraisers to establish the value of both properties. He also said I had the alternate option: to sell one or both of my homes. At the bottom of the letter, he copied James.

I could not afford to buy James out of either home. I would have to sell both.

When I read the letter, when I read James's texts, the world shifted. It became very dark.

My children were going to lose the house they loved, the center of our life as a family, and the apartment where they lived, in addition to managing the emotional toll of their father leaving. I was going to lose what my grandparents and my father had given me, betraying them too. I was going to lose my financial security.

There was no reason for it, given James's resources, given his desire to shed, given his refusal to make a home for the kids. It felt like he was playing a game, or running a deal, one he was going to win at all costs, by a wide margin, regardless of the impact on me and our children.

I fell into a deep well of despair and shame. I could no longer see the road ahead of me. I couldn't leave the house. I couldn't get out of bed. It was the same paralysis I'd felt in the first weeks after James left, but it felt much darker. When I closed my eyes, I saw myself hanging from the rafter in my bedroom. I could feel the cold metal of a gun against my temple. I imagined stepping off the tiles of my roof. I did not feel suicidal, I made no plans to hurt myself, but the images kept coming, rotating, like in a View-Master toy I'd had as a kid.

I texted my mother about what was happening, what I was seeing. I thought she would understand, having been through a depression in middle age, but I think I was really asking her to rescue me. I was scared. I didn't want to bother my psychiatrist while she was on vacation, away for the month of August.

Within an hour, my psychiatrist called me. My mother had tracked her down, terrified by what I had told her. My doctor put a name to what was happening—suicidal ideation. It could be sparked by intense stress and anxiety.

She said, "There is great emotional importance in a home. It is your history, your security, your identity, the way you shield and nurture your children. Losing your home will be deeply dislocating for you and the kids, as it is for many women going through divorce."

I said, "Other women face much more dire consequences. I should not complain." I had tried to have perspective, to see how privileged I still was, no matter what happened in the divorce. But my fear had made me myopic again, only able to see what I would lose.

She replied, "Belle, it is still a profound loss. Especially since the person you trusted most is on the other side." She continued, "The images you are seeing are an expression of agency, your brain giving you an escape hatch in the face of helplessness."

She put me on an antidepressant. Within a week, to my great relief, the images stopped. But the fear and shame remained.

———

During this dark, terrifying period, I still dreamt about James. In each dream, he appeared as the old version of him, as my kind and loving husband. I was so happy to see him, as he was to see me. We embraced, our hands joined, we kissed.

There were even sex scenes, skin on skin, his body returning to mine.

Sometimes I asked, "Where did you go?"

He answered, "I'm sorry. I don't know what happened."

I felt the sensation of letting go, the dissipation of the betrayal, the fear, the hurt, the relief.

When I woke up, my reality returned with a great thud.

I tried to will my brain to spare me from these dreams, to let go of my love, my longing, for this man who no longer existed.

———

As my lawyer and I prepared for trial, I told people what was at stake, what James was threatening. I did this in a desperate state, hoping someone, anyone, would intervene. My specific longing was for one of his male friends to take a stand, to say, *Do not do this to her. Do not do this to your kids.* I knew, in his world, the voice had to be male for it to land.

Instead, what I found, from some men, was a lack of concern, an acceptance of the state of things, a strong desire not to get involved. The message I received was that I should accept my fate; I should accept whatever James chose to give me. It felt like they were saying, *You've had a good run with your hedge fund husband. You should be grateful. It is time to pack your bags and go.*

At a dinner party in August, a man asked me how the divorce was going. I said, quietly, "Not well. It's brutal. He's trying to force me to sell my homes, which I bought." I was too raw then to censor myself, and I thought this man would be horrified by what I was telling him.

The man smiled widely and nodded. He said, "Ah, he's playing hardball!"

I thought, *Is this the game? Discard your wife and then give her as little as possible? Is this how these men impress one another?*

In late September, I learned that James was invited on a hunting weekend with a group of men I knew well, men whom I liked. I hadn't expected these men to cut James off; I knew it was better for all of us if James had friends. But including him at that moment, three weeks before our trial, knowing what he planned to do, shocked me. These men would drink with him, eat with him, chat with him, walk through the fields at dawn with guns in their hands.

I knew then: *He can do whatever he wants to me. He won't face any consequences.*

I was told that two of the men spoke to James over the weekend, encouraging him to be kind to me, but he returned from the trip even angrier, even more aggressive, as if the experience had refilled his tank, as if his basest intentions had been blessed.

I had several men in my life who stood up for me. A childhood friend, Evie's godfather, called me often, offering advice and support. Two other men on the Vineyard, a banker and a lawyer, tried to help me strategize, sharing insights about men in finance, about what matters to them and what doesn't.

My brother had been involved with the divorce from the beginning, lending his financial expertise, reading the counterclaim, interpreting James's spreadsheets. He was always calm, always reassuring me that things would work out fairly, encouraging me to move slowly, carefully. But when

James's plans were clear, my brother became distraught. His back went out and he couldn't move from his couch for two weeks. When his friends asked him what had happened, he answered, "My sister's divorce." He called and emailed me and my lawyer nearly every day, trying to come up with ideas to encourage, or force, James to settle.

Gradually, as the trial date approached, I started to accept what was going to happen. I started to imagine my life differently, the kids' lives differently. We would sell the house. We would move to a smaller apartment. I told myself every day, like a mantra, *I can do this. I can make a life for us.*

It helped to take responsibility for it. To see the moments, over twenty years, when I hadn't protected myself, when I had chosen comfort over conflict, not knowing over knowing. I had put myself here, one decision at a time.

I agreed to change the prenup, dismissing legal advice.

I put both our names on the deeds.

I chose not to be involved in our financial life.

I failed to make sure our prenup was extinguished.

I failed to think about what would happen if our marriage ended.

But I also tried to have compassion for the woman I was, agreeing to all of it, trusting my husband.

I did it for love. There is nothing shameful about that.

———

James and I reached a settlement an hour before our trial was set to begin, with terms determined by James. In our limited negotiations, by email, without our lawyers, I had to be calm, deferential, grateful. I had no wiggle room; he said if

I pushed him, if I enlisted the help of my lawyer, if I refused specific language, he would withdraw his offer and go to trial.

In the end, he gave up his interests in the house, the apartment, the beach, and the club. He pays me child support. He covers medical expenses and high-school tuition for the kids. He kept the money he accumulated during our marriage.

I don't know what finally made him decide to settle. I have several guesses, but I will never know for sure. Maybe he always planned to resolve it before trial, to give me the house and the apartment. But only after he brought me to my knees.

I give myself a lot of credit for the result, for weaving through the negotiations, for keeping my eyes on what I needed to keep my kids' lives stable, to keep what I cared about. I see the ending as a success. I have everything I need. I have everything that matters. I have plenty.

When I signed the agreement, I thought, *I will let this go now. I will not live in this conflict anymore.*

I was successful, for the most part, in letting it go. I don't think about the details of our divorce. I don't focus on what was lost.

What remains, what still brings a lump to my throat, a chill to my bones, is not about money.

It is the possibility that there was a timetable, a clock I didn't hear ticking.

It is his willingness to make me afraid when I was already devastated, already on the floor.

It is what he made clear within weeks of leaving, that he believed my contributions to his career, to our family, over twenty years, amounted to nothing.

———

After we settled, my lawyer helped me create a checklist of everything I had to do to separate myself from James financially. New checking accounts, a mortgage refinancing, registry applications for revised deeds, COBRA. It was a very long, very overwhelming list. James and I had created a complicated web over twenty years, with all strings leading back to him. I had to cut each string and begin again. I was overcome with anxiety. This is what I had feared. Understanding it. Doing it myself. Being responsible.

I chipped away at it. I created spreadsheets and budgets. I asked questions. I made myself understand it. I was pushy in making sure my mortgage refinancing closed at the locked-in rate. When I had to correspond with James about finances (or anything at all), I approached him as he had approached our divorce—emotionless, transactional.

Slowly, over many months, as my head came out of the sand, a form of joy set in—joy born of replacing the not knowing with knowing, the nub of worry with clarity, the lack of control with control. All made easier, of course, by the fact that I had enough to feel secure, to make my children secure.

I thought, *This is better than everything I lost. This is better than the life I thought I wanted.*

———

I took the memoir-writing class again in the spring of 2022. It was still on Zoom, once a week, from late February until late April. This time, I wrote for thirty minutes, at the same time every day, as the teacher instructed. At 6 a.m., after I woke Carrie and made her breakfast, I got my coffee, sat at my desk, and wrote. Thirty minutes grew to an hour, then two hours, then three. I wrote about my father's death, my stepfather, Rose. I liked the way it felt, sitting there, just me and the computer, working through things, crafting sentences, returning to each piece like they were friends or children who needed tending.

At the beginning of every class, the teacher asked if anyone wanted to read their work. A few people always volunteered. They read for three minutes and we clapped. During the second-to-last class, I raised my hand to read. I told myself I had to do it, I had to take this risk, to read my words.

I pulled up the essay I had written about James leaving. I knew I could get through half of it in three minutes. As I read, I tried to keep my voice even, but it wavered. My face grew hot, as it had when I was in school. When I was done, I closed the document and looked at my classmates. Everyone clapped. The teacher smiled from her square on the screen. I turned off my camera and microphone, went to my bathroom, and threw up. I read the second half of the piece the following week, during our last class.

I had written the essay in the format of "Modern Love," the *New York Times* column about relationships. I had loved the column since it first appeared in 2004. I knew the rhythm of the pieces, the flow, the punch at the end. I knew the word count.

The day the memoir class ended, two days before my fifty-second birthday, I submitted the piece to modernlove@

nytimes.com, their virtual slush pile. I titled it "And Then He Was Gone." I hadn't asked anyone to edit it. I wanted it to be all mine, to be exactly as I'd written it. I knew they received more than ten thousand submissions a year, even more during the pandemic. The chances of publication were less than one percent. Still, I pressed "Send."

———

I received our divorce decree in July 2022. I was on the Vineyard when it arrived in my email inbox. It was shocking to see our names again, the *v.* for him against me, the words ending our marriage. It was still painful to see James's choice on paper.

In the order, the judge granted me the right to return to my maiden name. I had to ask his permission. I understood why some of my friends kept their married names, the name their children had, after a divorce. But for me, changing my name felt like a public declaration, a before and after. As pieces of identification arrived in the mail—a new social security card, a new passport, new credit cards—I felt a rush of excitement and purpose. I was shedding my identity as James's wife. I was returning to who I had been before I was married. And I was adopting a new identity as a divorced woman, the label I never would have chosen on my own.

I still had two versions of that woman in my head: the undesirable, abandoned woman who sat in loneliness, who waited patiently for invitations from married couples, and the strong, independent one who decided how she would live her life, with whom she would spend her time, where she would go. A woman who would claim her role as her family's matriarch with pride, not shame. A woman who was no longer controlled or overshadowed by a man. I used Susan's spotlight trick again, forcing myself to shift the light from the first version to the second.

———

I ordered two new signs for our driveway: one with my last name and one with the kids' last name. It felt important to me—my renaming, the public statement of ownership. When the signs arrived, I could see that they were too big, almost obnoxious, but I felt a thrill once they were installed. I stood there for a long time, on the dirt road, looking at my name.

The Meadowpath sign James had nailed on the gate in 2006 was still there, the name we had adopted with such joy, the name that had symbolized all we had built together, the name appropriated from the original occupants of the land. I had left it there, thinking, *This is still our home. This is still what James and I created together.*

But then I thought. *No, it's not. It is not that anymore.*

I went back to the house, opened the junk drawer next to the fridge, and found a screwdriver. I walked back up the driveway and wedged it behind the sign, trying to pry it away. It wouldn't budge. I went back to the house and found a hammer. I returned to the gate and pounded the sign off. It dropped to the hard dirt of the driveway.

I carried the sign into the living room and stacked it on top of the wood in the fireplace. I was still using logs that

James had chopped two years before, when I clung to him during the frightening first days of the pandemic, a mix of blueberry, oak, and pine. I lit a match and set fire to all of it.

That year, I let the paths of our woods become padded with leaves, with poison ivy, with pine needles and brush. I let the trees on the edge of the lawn grow in. The overgrowth was a daily reminder of James's absence, of the loss of his care and tending. But it was beautiful, in its own way, the growing in, the wildness.

———

I threw a big party at the end of July. It was not a divorce celebration; I did not think my divorce was anything to celebrate. But I wanted to welcome all the people who had been kind to me, and the few who hadn't. I wanted to make it clear that I had survived my calamity. When my guests drove in, they saw my maiden name on the gate. There could be no uncertainty about who would stay, about who would disappear.

———

The Chilmark Road Race takes place every August on the island. It is a five-kilometer race on a famously beautiful road with open horse pastures, classic Chilmark rock walls, shading oak trees. It is a community event, with participants ranging from newborns being pushed in their strollers to senior citizens. Residents line the course to cheer, holding homemade signs, manning water tables, spraying hoses to cool down runners. Participants wear race T-shirts dating back to 1978, the year the race was launched to benefit the Chilmark

Community Center. Participation is a labor of love—to get to the starting line, runners must take a bus, walk a stretch, and wait, often for almost an hour, for the race to begin. While the course is bucolic and fairly short, it is not easy—there are several gradual, torturous hills.

I started running in the race in 2014 and returned every year. I loved it—the community spirit, bumping into people I hadn't seen all summer, collecting my bibs like prizes. I brought each of the kids once, Finn when he was twelve, the girls at fourteen and eleven, all enthusiastic until they encountered the hills.

Before 2020, I ran regularly over the summer. I always felt ready for the race once the second Saturday in August rolled around. But after James left, I stopped running. It felt too harsh, requiring too much energy, too much of me. I'd walked the eight-mile loop around Vineyard Haven, but I never ran again, not even a jog.

The race had been canceled in 2020 for the pandemic and I skipped it in 2021, when I was in the middle of the divorce, when I felt so fragile. In August 2022, after my divorce was final, after I'd changed my name, after the fear had dissipated, I did the race again. I went by myself, sitting on the bus alone, standing in the crowd at the starting line, feeling anxious, wondering if I would be able to do it, if I would make it up the hills, if I could finish.

But as I ran, as I encountered each hill, as I plodded slowly up the gradual slopes, I felt steady, solid. My breath was even. I didn't worry about all the people passing me. I told myself any finish time was fine, as long as I didn't stop.

To my amazement, I beat all my previous times. All the walking, miles and miles over two years, must have increased my endurance. Without intending to, I had made myself stronger.

———

My law partner and I took on another immigration case. We were representing our first male client, a fourteen-year-old boy. His mother had died when he was two. He had been physically and emotionally abused by his father. He had been forced to miss school to work in their fields. He had been harassed, chased, and beaten by local gangs. At thirteen, he traveled by bus and train toward the United States, eventually crossing the border by foot. He was detained by border agents and released with a USCIS hearing date. He took a bus to New York, where he was welcomed by his maternal aunt.

Neither my partner nor I speak Spanish, so we engaged a friend of hers, another former corporate lawyer, to translate. We conducted interviews, all slower with translation, and prepared his documents. We appeared at our client's USCIS hearing and filed his paperwork in family court.

There was something different about working with a boy. I thought about Finn often, about James, about the difficult road from boyhood to manhood. I thought, again, about the power of putting words to experiences, especially traumatic ones, and the power of personal narrative. I had done it for myself, in my counterclaim and my essay, and for my clients in the paperwork we filed in court, but not for James. I had

stopped trying to see his whole story, the pieces that made
the man he had become.

———

After James picked up the boxes I'd opened and retaped in
the spring of 2020, I went through the basement, trying to
organize the mess. I skirted mice droppings and cobwebs as I
crawled on the cold concrete floor and pulled bins from the
wooden shelves. I went through the banker boxes Susan had
given me from the house in Water Mill—my father's documents from his time on the city council, his campaign mem-
orabilia, his college thesis on Henry Miller. I found remnants
of my childhood—a diary from third grade that was exces-
sively cheerful, even about Rose, as if I thought someone
would read it. There were several journals from trips to Europe with my father and Susan, my loopy childhood print
reviewing the food, décor, service, and bathrooms of every
restaurant we went to. I pulled out the uniform skirt I'd
worn on my last day of ninth grade, signed by my classmates
in blue ballpoint pen. I found stacks of handwritten letters
from Lynn and Anna, sent to me every summer, long before email existed. There were several boxes of *Archie* comic
books, their covers faded.

I found the red diary James and I used to document our
love affair in 1998, our tiny print in pencil, alternating each
day, from him to me. I found our wedding album on a shelf,
wrapped in a dish towel. I'd placed it there in March 2020,
one of the items that was too painful to look at after James
left. There were objects that tracked the growth of our
family—Finn's first shoes (red leather with Velcro straps), the

puffy pink snowsuit both girls wore home from the hospital, dozens of paintings from the years of art classes on our lawn, papier-mâché birds and family portraits from their days in elementary school. I found hockey helmets and ice skates, Christmas decorations, wooden sleds, the framed map of James and Evie's epic walk in Rome.

From a high shelf, I pulled down plastic bins of photographs, the extra prints I hadn't taped into our albums, loose ones from my childhood and James's. I looked through the images of both of us, small color prints and larger black-and-white portraits. I saw myself as a shy little girl with big eyes, always watching, always a little bit scared. I saw James as a surprisingly large baby (his mother had told me he refused baby food, grabbing hamburgers from her hand at six months old), as a child of ten, a towhead with a mischievous grin, on the dig in Crete as a high-school student, writing in a journal, his skin golden brown, his hair nearly white.

When I looked at the photographs of James at eight, ten, twelve, I saw Finn, the resemblance strong at every age. I also saw a child, a boy, his parents' beloved, wild middle son. That child had been changed by what had happened to his father, by the story no one spoke about. That child had lived with a pervasive fear of financial ruin, of never having enough, from an age before puberty. That child felt a crushing comparison to his friends with easy wealth, who never had to worry. That child had lost the house he loved. That child had worried for decades about both his parents, about his own survival. That child grew into a man who was still scared. That child grew into a man who could leave his family without explaining why, maybe without knowing why.

That child grew into a man who would fight fiercely to keep what he believed was his.

I felt a rush of something—not quite tenderness, but an understanding. James's need to protect himself existed long before he had met me, long before I walked into his office with my Oscar ballot. If what happened in our divorce was vengeance, it was an existential vengeance, not a personal one. It had very little to do with me. And it existed on another plane from our love story.

———

In February 2023, nine months after I submitted my essay to "Modern Love," I emailed the slush pile address again, asking if they could let me know if it was a rejection. I got an email from the senior editor of the column the next day. He wrote that they were considering it for publication.

I was elated.

I called my mother and Susan. They reacted almost identically—with great excitement for me, about my return to writing, about the opening of something new after my heartbreak, about the validation. They loved the piece. But their excitement was quickly followed by fear. They were scared that James would be angry and retaliate if I published it. They worried about me putting something so personal out into the world.

My mother asked, "Can he unwind your settlement?"

Susan said, "You've come so far since then. You are not just this story anymore."

My mother and Susan are both strong, outspoken women, but publishing something like this, about your husband leaving you, was not something they would do. My mother had never spoken about her ex-partner's multiple infidelities. Susan had covered for my father's temper, for his pills, for his debt. We had all been taught to fill in the hole that men left, to be quiet about men behaving badly, to move on with grace. Publishing an account of what happened to me was shining a light on that hole, the deep crevice James had left. I was refusing something—the cleaning up, the grace.

My grandmother was still appearing in my dreams. I still woke up thinking about her. She had been devastated that a story about her husband's affair had been made public. I wondered, *Would she be horrified by this? Horrified by me?*

I paused. I showed the piece to the kids. I spoke to my lawyer. And then I decided to go ahead.

———

The editor of "Modern Love" and I went back and forth over email, working on my piece. The word count for publication was lower than the one allowed for submissions. We disagreed on some things. I held firm on language I wanted to stay. In March, we were close to finalizing the draft.

Then, by email, he told me that I needed to show the essay to James "to get his reaction." He said that the standards editor of the paper required it. James was not named in the piece, but he was easily identifiable with one Google search—our wedding announcement had been published in the *Times* in 1999. When the editor first contacted me, he told me that James would receive a fact-check call. I hadn't understood that he would need to approve the piece as a whole, or I had missed it, this critical step in the process.

I wrote to the editor, "It seems like such a rule would silence many women writing about their own experience of an event." I didn't recognize this version of myself— a woman challenging a respected male editor.

He responded, "Showing him the essay and considering his response would be the beginning of the process, not the end." In our exchange, the editor described my piece as "your account." Suddenly, I felt doubted. Like what I had written might not be true. Like I could have made it all up.

I knew how it would play out. James would object, not to the substance (he could not contest the facts of it), but globally, to being written about at all. And the *Times* would drop the piece. They would not risk a lawsuit, especially when the subject was a wealthy man, a former lawyer. If this was the likely result, I could not risk inflaming him again.

I told the editor we were at an impasse. I could not elicit James's reaction. He said he understood, but they would not change their process.

I had reached the end of the road. I had tried. The editor had thought it was good enough to publish and that would have to be enough.

———

I saw James again at Evie's graduation from boarding school in May 2023. She was allowed to have as many guests as she wanted. We no longer needed to wear masks. I did not wear black. It was a beautiful day.

When James arrived in his suit and tie, striding across the lawn, I noted that the rush of longing was still there, but it was brief, fleeting, nearly imperceptible. As we sat side by side in our row of folding chairs, I did not have any desire to hold his hand. My body was finally catching up.

———

In June 2023, my desire to publish my story did not go away. I could not let it go. It was the same feeling I had before filing my losing counterclaim—a rebelliousness, a desire to reclaim something that was mine, an internal drive to abandon the quiet, the submissiveness, that had not served me. I also knew, in my gut, that it had a greater purpose. *This is going to help someone.*

And I liked the essay. I had worked on it for more than a year. I wanted it to be read.

As I walked the West Side Highway, I thought, *I am allowing myself to be silenced again. By a man.*

And then, *I have to send it to James. There is no other way.*

I emailed James, "I've started writing again and it has been helpful to me. I wrote a piece about our divorce which I would like to publish. Do you want to read it?"

He said yes. I sent it.

He didn't answer for ten days. I wrote to him again.

He answered, "I haven't been able to bring myself to read it. Are you critical of me?"

Before I could respond, he texted, "Your article is good, sad, hard to read, I'm supportive."

I was stunned. I don't know why he approved it. He may not have seen anything wrong with the story—a man was allowed to leave in the way he did. Or, maybe, possibly, he wanted to help me.

I took a screenshot of James's text and sent it to the

"Modern Love" editor. We spoke on the phone for the first time, for over an hour. He was kind and compassionate. He said he wanted me to add a line about my current contact with James. He was still concerned about being fair to him. He asked, "How about, 'We are in touch about arrangements for the kids'?"

I said, "Remember, there aren't any arrangements. I have the kids all the time."

He was stunned. Even in his compassion, even having edited my story, he had not quite believed it.

He said he would publish the piece in two weeks.

———

The essay went online at midnight on June 30, 2023. It would run in the hard copy of the Sunday paper on July 2.

I was on the Vineyard. The kids were away. Evie was traveling with friends. Carrie was on a teen tour. Finn had started a summer internship with a real estate firm. I sat in the living room in my pajamas and socks, in the chair by the fireplace where Carrie had sat upside down telling me she knew about her father's affair. The dog slept on the floor next to me. I reloaded the page and waited for the essay to appear.

And then there it was. My name and my words in print. The artwork showed me in a dress looking at James on an island; the background was a dark pink, my favorite color when I was a kid. The editor had given the piece a new title: "Was I Married to a Stranger?"

I sat with the piece on my screen, by myself, for over an hour.

It was thrilling.

And then, like the moment I placed baby Evie on the floor in the same room, I thought, *What have I done?*

———

I had seen publication as a finish line. I didn't imagine anything after that. And somehow, I had not understood that I was putting both my story and my writing into the world for judgment.

Friends on the West Coast who were still awake, most of them college classmates who worked in the entertainment industry, texted me. They said that they loved it. They said they loved the writing.

I slept for a few hours and woke up to more emails and texts. Friends posted it on Instagram. Joyce Carol Oates, a regular reader of "Modern Love," tweeted it. Two editors at big publishing houses reached out to say how good they thought it was. Their approval, as arbiters of good writing, shook me. I thought, *Maybe Greg was wrong?*

My closest friends, my family, the people who had lived through the ordeal with me, who had called and texted me every day, were ebullient. They had seen me at my lowest; they had talked to me from the bathroom floor, from my bed, when I couldn't get up. This rising was, to them, beautiful and just.

My mother wrote, "You have spoken for so many women, including me, who have suffered the consequences of ruthless male prerogative and behavior. No more shutting up women about what men have always gotten away with. Rebirth! New life! I am so proud!"

I went out on the lawn with the dog, lying beside him

on the cold, wet grass. When I looked up at the sky, at the house, I saw a swarm of dragonflies, dozens of them, moving as a mass from the roof to the pool, to me, and back again. I had never seen anything like it. They didn't buzz, they vibrated, a ball of energy three feet wide, circling above me.

Later, I googled "swarm of dragonflies," wondering if it signified something wrong with the house, with the ecosystem of the land. I found an answer I wasn't expecting, from several sites. Dragonflies did not indicate danger. They were symbolic of self-actualization.

It was then that I said to myself, *This is what was meant to happen. This was the only way I could get here.*

———

Over the next few days, I received more than a hundred texts and emails, some sent to me directly, some forwarded from the "Modern Love" inbox. Both men and women thanked me for writing the essay. Many wrote that the same thing had happened to them, or something similar—an abandonment, a lack of warning or explanation, gaslighting. One woman wrote, "Ms. Burden's essay made *me* feel less alone—so she has, in fact, made a difference in my life." Another wrote, "For many of us who have uncovered secret lives of our husbands/partners, experienced being cut off and gaslighting when trying to seek answers and understanding—it is a lonely club and a situation where it is very difficult to avoid feeling shame." A man wrote, "A huge thank you, Belle, for this article. I, too, lived a similar experience and reading your piece on living with a stranger filled me with a sense of comfort. I appreciate the sharing of your experience, and please know, you have helped others."

Some readers tried to help me understand what had happened. One reader alerted me to the phenomenon of "runaway husbands," men who leave their wives without warning or explanation. Another reader, a woman, wrote, "I think that the reason you didn't know who your husband was, is because he is not really able to deal with contradictions or uncertainties within himself. Therefore, he could be the Rebel, the Loyal Husband, and then the I Must Break Free to Be Myself Betrayer." Her analysis felt true, even though she had never met James.

As the emails came in, I felt steadier in my decision to publish. I had made other people feel seen and acknowledged, and they had done the same for me. We had made each other feel less alone.

It wasn't all positive. One woman wrote, "This seemed like more of a roast and 'outing' of her former spouse. Honestly just mean." Another woman, a lawyer, addressed the impact on my children: "Belle, there is no excuse for you to involve your children publicly in the failure of your marriage." One reader wrote, "I have to say this story is so polished it's totally unbelievable."

The article was reposted on online blogs, which looked like organized forums for bashing me. They did not hold back. I was called a "rich bitch" who "deserved to be left." I was "ugly," "fat," a "hausfrau." James was the hero, a man leaving an unhappy marriage to an awful person. One man posted that my writing was so bad, he couldn't finish reading the essay.

Two days after my piece appeared online, the *Daily Mail*

posted an article about me. Within a few hours, it rose to the top of their website. I had not anticipated this, but I probably should have. It listed my parents, my grandparents, the bold names, the ancestry of privilege. I was mortified. The way it was written made my story, my decision to publish, seem tawdry, vindictive, sad. I knew the *Daily Mail* article would come up whenever you googled me, for the rest of my life, right after my wedding announcement.

———

The timing of the article's publication coincided exactly with the start of summer at the tennis club. I felt as vulnerable as I had in 2020, putting on my sneakers, making myself walk the club's loop, not allowing myself to hide. I knew I was the subject of conversation. I knew the article was being forwarded around by text. I knew there would be opinions.

Three years earlier, in my rawness, I had been ultrasensitive to other people's reactions to me, to the news of James leaving. I was buoyed and crushed in equal measure. And here I was, back in the same position. But this time, I had chosen it. This time, I had put myself in this place. This time, my fear of how people would react was dusted with something else: excitement, pride.

As in my darkest days, I was greeted with a lot of kindness. People went out of their way to stop me on the road, at cocktail parties. They sent congratulatory texts. They said they thought I was brave to do it. They said they loved the piece, the writing. All generations reached out, the oldest club members, the youngest teenagers. I nearly wept when they did. When they extended a hand.

But, as in 2020, I felt an undercurrent, a shadow, a different view.

Several men I knew well didn't say anything to me about the article at all. I sensed a palpable discomfort, a desire to avoid me, like I was suddenly radioactive. Maybe these men hadn't read the essay, maybe they had and were horrified, maybe they thought it was unfair to James, even though I had done everything possible to soften it. I didn't know.

On the dock in the late afternoon, a man asked me if I had planted the *Daily Mail* article.

I was astonished. "No, of course not!"

He shrugged and turned away.

———

The day the print version of the article appeared in the paper, I met a close friend at the clothing store where many women bought their summer dresses. She was tall, lithe, her hair in a pixie cut. She was in the dressing room when I arrived. I drew back the curtain a few inches. She looked stressed. She said, "I have to tell you, people are really gossiping about the article."

"What are they saying?" I asked.

She pulled a flowered dress over her head. She said, "I don't want to tell you."

I answered, "Come on. You have to tell me. And you have to tell me who is saying it." I felt a fierceness rising in me, in defense of myself.

She listed a series of married names, all club members. As I heard each name, I felt like I was being stung—once, twice, three times.

She said, "They don't understand why you would do it. They are shocked you would do it. It *is* shocking."

I had always liked this friend's honesty, her bluntness, and I liked that we sparred sometimes. She had been firmly supportive of me after James's exit, never wavering. I knew I could have this conversation with her and still feel safe.

She continued, "I told them you did it because you wanted to be a writer."

"That's not why I did it."

She stepped into another dress. "Well, I also said it was cathartic for you to write about it."

I'd heard the word *cathartic* several times. It felt demeaning, like I just needed to get my anger out of my system and then I would shut up. I don't think anyone would have used the word to explain the motives of a male writer.

I said, "There are many easier ways to feel catharsis than trying to get published."

She answered, "Then why? Everyone thinks it's for revenge."

Revenge felt even more demeaning than *catharsis*. It erased every other reason a woman might want to tell her story, every artistic purpose, and reduced it to only one thing: getting back at the man who had rejected her. The "Modern Love" editor had told me they never publish pieces that ring of bitterness or vengeance. He said he had picked mine because it was not that. I had worked hard to remove any anger from the story, to keep my tone even and fair.

Still, I'd asked myself, *Am I doing this to hurt James?* I'd wanted James to understand what had happened after he left, to see the impact, to see me. *But isn't that different from revenge?*

In the store, I felt hot with anger. I was being shamed instead of celebrated on the day I first held my published article in my hand. I was being criticized for writing an honest account of what had happened to me and my kids. By my own community, by people I knew.

I dropped the curtain and walked out.

In my car, I tried to calm down. I knew my friend was the messenger of something I had felt but couldn't identify—the counterview in the air. It was helpful to know exactly what was being said. And I should have expected it.

These are people who do not speak about private things.

These are people who do not air their dirty laundry.

———

A week later, during cocktails before a dinner party, another friend pulled me to the corner of the room. She was younger than I was and very kind. She whispered the name of another married mother at the club. "She's saying terrible things about you. It's so upsetting."

I sighed. "What is she saying?"

My friend's eyes darted around the room, making sure no one was listening. "She's talking about you as a mother. Saying that a good mother wouldn't do this. They wouldn't do it to their children."

I knew this was a possibility, this view. But it still felt like a punch to the softest part of me. *Bad mother*. A good mother is meant to protect her kids at all costs. A good mother would never call out her children's father publicly.

I didn't answer my friend. I didn't try to defend myself. My fire was gone. I couldn't find any words that would absolve me.

———

As the summer progressed, I continued to absorb people's reactions. The cloud of hurt threatened to consume me again, the sinking feeling that I would be alienated, judged, excluded. It felt so familiar, a particular pain that highlighted all I had lost, all that was missing, all that was wrong with me. In the dark of the night, I was my own harshest critic: *You have embarrassed yourself. You are a selfish, vengeful person. You are a bad mother.*

But in the morning, as I walked the loop I'd mapped in 2020, I was able to steer myself through it again, through the noise and opinions, reminding myself why I wrote the piece, why it mattered, why it wasn't wrong.

I could see that the voice in my head, the one shaming me, had been there since I was a little girl, warning me against speaking up, especially about a man. I could see that the voice was sexist. I could see that it was silencing.

I could see that some people, both online and in person, were uncomfortable with me coming out of my lane, a place where women stayed quiet, where men are allowed to do what serves them, no matter what the wreckage. I could see they were defending something bigger, a way of life, the safety it gave them.

I could see that when I was told I was too upset, too hurt,

too open—words used against me since the first days after James's departure—it shifted the narrative. Once a woman is painted as a hysteric, the rest of the story is washed away.

I could see that many of my detractors had said nothing to me about James leaving. To them, a woman writing about a man leaving is, somehow, worse than the man leaving.

I started to tell myself what I should have known from the beginning: *Some people will root for me. Some won't.*

When I wrestled with the harshest judgment leveled at me, the labeling of me as a bad mother, another voice started to emerge:

What if telling the story publicly, saying what happened to us, actually helps my kids? What if seeing their mother rise, seeing her claim her life, giving clarity to their experience, is the greater gift?

Isn't this possible too?

———

In the fall, I started digitizing the movies James had made of our family. There were sixteen DVDs, each in a case with images of the kids on the cover. I wanted the kids to have permanent copies, especially as DVD players became obsolete.

I watched the movies before converting them. They tell the story of every year since Finn was born, every holiday, every vacation, every summer on the Vineyard. James rarely shows up in them; he is usually the one filming. He talks from behind the camera. There is a sweetness to his presence, watching over us, encouraging us. But there is something melancholy about it too. I can see that he was most comfortable at a remove, at a distance.

I felt a deep longing as I watched the movies, for those years with the kids, for their innocence, for the endless days I often dragged myself through, for all that slipped through my fingers. But I felt joy too, watching our family, the moments of pure, authentic happiness, the way James, even at a distance, is adoring of us, lingering on each member of his family—four-year-old Finn running down Chambers Street in a Batman costume, Evie smiling from her crib, Carrie covered in Mardi Gras beads in New Orleans. And me, carrying babies, cooking dinner, swimming in the ocean.

The movies feel like love.

A friend once asked what I would do with our wedding album, would I throw it away? Another friend asked if I had to rethink my memories with James, if his ultimate betrayal had cast a shadow over all that came before?

Even in my lowest moments, even in the nadirs of hurt and betrayal, I still believed in our love story, in our happiness as a family. Those stories are preserved in the words we wrote to each other, in the movies James made, in the albums I made, in the life we collected over the years. But they also exist in our kids' minds, in their skin and bones, in their souls. And in mine. James changed our present and our future, but not our past. This is the gift of an abrupt departure, an exit with no lead-up or warning. He didn't infect our lives with discord, with bickering, with visible discontent, before he left. He kept it lovely until he blew it up.

So, I answer, *No, I will not throw our wedding album away. No, I do not rethink our memories together. They are true. And they are ours.*

Part V

After spending the winter apart, the male and female ospreys return to their breeding ground, to the nest they built. The male arrives first, claiming their home, rebuilding and adding material. When the female appears, he courts her again, sky-dancing, fishing, feeding her after her long journey. They become reacquainted, preparing, together, for a new summer, for new life.

The couple's grown offspring are on their own, staying near the equator for another year, eventually flying north, perhaps to find their own mates, to build their own nests, on another island, at the edge of another lake.

———

I never got the answers I wanted.

I know James has not remarried. I know he is still a partner at the hedge fund in Nolita. I know he travels a lot. I know that he sees the kids for occasional dinners, tennis matches, and Rangers games. I know he is kind and loving with them, while sticking to his initial decision about co-parenting—there have been no overnights, vacations, or holidays since the day he left.

I don't know how long he stayed with the woman with the alliterative name, or if she is still in his life. I don't know if he cheated throughout our marriage or if she was his first and only affair. I don't know if he made the decision to leave suddenly after being caught, or if he'd carefully planned his exit for years. I don't know what role the pandemic played. I don't know how much of it was about money. I don't know how much of it was about me.

I don't know why he left. I don't think I ever will.

I still think, maybe, there will be a final act in the play, an end to the story, when I am given my answer. But the years go by without one. There is only silence.

———

In early October of 2023, I was walking with a friend, passing the subway station near the Brooklyn Bridge, the exit James and I had used on our first date. It was late morning. It was warm, nearly seventy degrees, with rain threatening.

I heard my name, yelled loudly, "Belle, Belle!"

I looked around, unable to locate the source. Then I saw a man across the street, on a narrow strip of sidewalk separating the road from the pedestrian entrance to the bridge. He was tall, handsome, dressed in a black sweater, tan corduroys, orange sneakers, his hair a mix of blond and gray. He was smiling widely and waving his arm high, back and forth, like a long-lost friend. It was James.

I slowed my pace. I smiled. I waved. I said, "Hi."

Then I turned from him, resuming my path forward, rejoining my friend who was a few steps ahead. I could see from the corner of my eye that he was still standing there, his arm raised, watching me walk away.

When I think of James now, I think of that man waving. He is not a villain. He is a man with his own wounds. He is my children's father, the source of many years of love and happiness. He is someone who made decisions about his own life, his own future. He is someone I can survive without. He is someone I don't know. He is someone who doesn't know me.

———

My daughters still crawl into bed with me, even at sixteen and nineteen. They still wear monkey-print pajamas. They still wake up with their hair tousled from sleep. Carrie looks like my mother and has her fierceness, her drive. Evie has my grandmother's frame and a lot of Susan's personality. They also look like James's side of the family. They are a mix of all the women who came before them. Finn now looks like a combination of his father and my father, and some of me, his own legacy. If I have grandchildren, they will be a mix too, of James and me, and all that came before.

One summer morning, the girls and I lay in my bed, the same one I had such trouble getting out of in the spring of 2020 and the summer of 2021. Finn sat in the blue upholstered chair in the corner of the room. Our dog, still sweet and still difficult, lay at his feet, gnawing on a stuffed reindeer we'd given him for Christmas.

Carrie said, "I miss us as a family."

I answered, "Me too." I paused. "But we are good now too, don't you think?"

Evie lay her head on my shoulder. She said, "Yes. We are good."

Carrie said, "I guess. I just wish . . . I wish I was little again."

I kissed the back of her head. I said, "I know."

As my children lay around me, I felt their steady growth to adulthood, to womanhood and manhood, an unstoppable force. I think a lot about the relationships ahead of them, about their eventual choice of life partners. *Will they repeat patterns because of what is ingrained in their biology? Because of what they saw? Will they attract partners who betray them, like me, my mother, my grandmother? Will they leave their marriages in middle age, failing to warn or explain? Or, maybe, because I talked about it, because I wrote about it, because I didn't pretend it was okay, I have stopped something?*

Maybe this is what my grandmother was whispering in my ear.

Be brave. Claim it. Say it. Break the cycle.

I hope because I was open about what happened to me, my children will insist on intimacy, on knowing their partner deeply, on being known deeply. I hope they will talk to their partners about money, about what will happen if the partnership ends. I hope that as they build trust in their relationships, they never lose sight of their own authority, their own voice, their own intuition. I hope they will move toward people who are in pain, rather than away. I hope they will understand that every person has experiences that make them who they are. I hope they will fall in love with abandon as I did with their father. I hope they will know, from watching me, that if everything falls apart, they can get up and piece together something new.

———

The summer my divorce was final, the osprey pole began to tilt under the nest's weight, leaning slightly to the left, toward the house. The birds were still in it, perhaps oblivious to the danger. It looked like the pole could come crashing down at any moment or, more likely, fall slowly, imperceptibly, into the marsh.

After the ospreys left in the fall, the osprey experts righted the pole and added reinforcing planks to its base. They used a chain saw to cut the nest, removing more than three feet of height. The nest was now flat and tidy, no longer decorated with haphazard twigs, with strands of colored string.

I worried the couple would never return to the nest in its new state. It was too stripped down. They would find a different home. I would have to wait for another pair to adopt the nest, to adopt us.

But a year later, I saw the birds' silhouettes in the nest. I walked through the woods, down the paths covered with leaves, over Carrie's rock, past the log carved with Evie's initials, and out to the end of the boardwalk. I crossed the beach named for Finn and stepped into the marsh, my sneakers sinking in the soft ground, coming closer to the pole. I looked up at the ospreys and waved. With a full voice, I said, "Welcome home."

ACKNOWLEDGMENTS

My agent, Brettne Bloom, believed in this book from the very beginning, found the perfect home for it, and held my hand for the last two and a half years as I wrote it, revised it, and launched it. She is the best reader, thought partner, adviser, protector, and friend. The greatest gift of this experience is knowing her.

My editor, Whitney Frick, gave me the structure for the book, edited it with a laser sharp eye, and guided me through the process with clear vision and unwavering support. She is an extraordinary editor and publisher. I'm honored to have her imprint on these pages.

I am thankful to the The Dial Press team, including Avideh Bashirrad, Debbie Aroff, Michelle Jasmine, Talia Cieslinski, Corina Diaz, Donna Cheng, Aarushi Menon, Barbara Bachman, Andy Lefkowitz, Rebecca Berlant, Sandra Sjursen, Mark McCauslin, Random House publisher Andy Ward, and the many others behind the scenes who turned my pages into something beautiful and expertly guided this book into the world.

My thanks to Jenny Meyer, the best of foreign agents, and everyone at The Book Group.

I'm so grateful to the editors of "Modern Love" for setting all of this in motion, to Lizzie Simon for her writing class and her encouragement, and to Isabel Gillies for welcoming me so warmly into the genre she pioneered.

Suzan Bellincampi, naturalist, writer, and Islands Director, Mass Audubon, and Steve Allen, Felix Neck Wildlife Sanctuary volunteer, shared their extensive knowledge about Martha's Vineyard ospreys and reviewed my text for accuracy. I thank them for their help and for all they do to protect the island's wildlife.

I am so lucky to work with my law partner, Nancy Bynum, our clients, their families, and Safe Passage Project. The legal work described in the book took place between 2020 and 2023. The landscape has changed significantly since then, becoming far more challenging, unpredictable, and dehumanizing. Nancy and I continue to advocate for our clients to the best of our abilities.

Marilyn Chinitz, Ory Appelboim, Anna Fels, Wendy Holmes, and Eric Rayman helped me in more ways than I can count. I am so fortunate to have them in my corner.

I have so many incredible friends who supported me during the writing of this book and the events recounted in it. They know who they are. But a special thank-you to Laurisa Schutt and Carin Giddings, my sisters in arms, my touchpoints, my early-morning and late-night rescuers. I would not be where I am now, or the person I am now, without them. I am also grateful to Rachel Bachner, Susie Gilbert,

Billy Lehmberg, Marlane Melican, David Netto, and Eliza Paolucci for reading early drafts and giving me the courage to keep going.

My thanks and love always to D, P, and E.

My brother and sister-in-law, Carter and Charmaine Burden, always show up exactly when I need them. They are wise and loving beyond measure.

My stepmother, Susan Burden, has been with me from the first phone call to the final draft, and every moment in between. She is the reason I could stand up after each wave knocked me down. I thank my lucky stars that she agreed to go out with my father fifty-two years ago. This is her book too.

My mother, Amanda Burden, has been my greatest supporter. Her belief in this book and in me has meant more than I can ever fully express.

My kids make every day of my life better. They are the kindest people I know. I thank them for absolutely everything. They will want me to thank our very sweet dog, Charlie Blue, too.

ABOUT THE AUTHOR

BELLE BURDEN is a pro bono immigration attorney specializing in juvenile cases. Her writing has appeared in *The New York Times*. She lives with her children in New York City.

ABOUT THE TYPE

This book was set in Bembo, a typeface based on
an old-style Roman face that was used for
Cardinal Pietro Bembo's tract *De Aetna* in 1495.
Bembo was cut by Francesco Griffo (1450–1518) in
the early sixteenth century for Italian Renaissance
printer and publisher Aldus Manutius (1449–1515).
The Lanston Monotype Company of Philadel-
phia brought the well-proportioned letterforms
of Bembo to the United States in the 1930s.